AMERICAN RONIN: THE WAY OF WALKING ALONE

A COMMENTARY ON MIYAMOTO MUSASHI'S
<u>DOKKODO</u>

D1105926

BY
JOSEPH HALL

FOREWORD BY

SCOTT CUNNINGHAM

Man, if someone has to tell you that martial arts and weight training can be dangerous then I don't think telling you here does any good either. But the lawyers say we have to so:

Library of Congress cataloguing in process.

ISBN:

For Amanda

PREFACE AND APOLOGY:

When I wrote this slender volume, it was my hope and intention that it might possess value for every man and not just for veterans of the recent wars. My own experience has been shaped largely by my time and training as an infantryman and then a medic in the US Army, a police officer, a Border Patrol Agent and a Federal Air Marshal and, as a natural result, perhaps, it too often sounds as if I would dismiss the experience, training, and virtue of men who have never lifted a sword or a handgun in service to the state.

Now, I beg your indulgence, I beg your understanding, I beg, even, your forgiveness if this seems the case.

If you are a man who values prowess and honor and The Good and have ever closed your fist in training or in battle, or even considered that one day your life might end defending what you hold more dear, then I wrote this commentary for you.

FOREWORD

All men may be created equal, but they are not all created the same. Prepare to take a look into the mindset of a man who walks the warrior path. For those who walk a similar path, these words will be familiar. For those unaccustomed to this mindset, what you are about to read may be unsettling. Clear your mind. Prepare to have your beliefs, perceptions, and opinions challenged. Not all that you will read will be agreeable or comforting. That's not the intent. Reading should not be about finding happy conformity, rather about shining a light into the shadows of our minds to illuminate things we have never confronted. The purpose of these words is not to bring comfort. Instead, they are meant to illuminate. To cast a light onto ideas and thoughts that you yourself may never have come to on your own.

Hopefully this work will allow for a better understanding of those who walk the Warrior's Path. Unlike the Vietnam vets who were rejected, the modern veterans are respected by society. That does not mean that they are understood. The warrior code is foreign to most civilians, and even when explained, it is seen as foreign and frightening.

Our perceptions are shaped by our experiences. Joe Hall has probably experienced life far differently than you. To find that his perception differs from yours should be no surprise. I have known Joe for two decades. In this times have found that the heart of a warrior beats in his chest. He lives his life through dedication, training, and discipline. He sees the world as he does without apology or excuse. Challenge his views. He expects no less, since this is the path he has chosen. But, when you do, challenge him with logic and reason, not emotion or instinct.

Many who live in Western societies go through life experiencing the world as they wish it to be, rather than how it is. This is possible because they are guarded by men of action who not only accept the world the way it is, but thrive in the challenge. The notion that humans are not predisposed to violence is unsupported by fact. Humans will attempt as much violence as they see necessary in order to achieve their selfish goals. The only reliable guard against this is not slogans, or social pressure, but the threat of violent consequence. While you may find this warrior ethos and outlook harsh, drastic, and coldly pragmatic, it is actually a historical norm...warriors are necessary for the survival of nations, societies, and cultures. Be thankful that there are men prepared to use violence on our behalf.

Now, prepare for a look into the way one of these men looks at the world around him.

Scott Cunningham
Summer 2018

(NOTE: Scott Cunningham was my Squadron Commanding Officer for years, including our deployment to Afghanistan when he was also the

6

Coalition Forces Commander for Laghman Province. He is one of the last classically trained warriors on the government payroll and one of the few men I've met who is obviously smarter than I am. It's a cliché to say I'd follow him to hell, but I kept all my fire retardant uniforms just in case. I rode with the Wildhorse. I rode with Scott Cunningham. -The Author)

THE DOKKODO

PRECEPT ONE: Accept things exactly as they are.

PRECEPT TWO: Do not seek pleasure for its own sake.

PRECEPT THREE: Do not ever rely on a partial feeling.

PRECEPT FOUR: Think lightly of yourself but seriously of the world.

PRECEPT FIVE: Avoid attachment to desire for as long as you live.

PRECEPT SIX: Do not regret anything that you have done.

PRECEPT SEVEN: Never be envious.

PRECEPT EIGHT: Never let yourself be saddened by a separation.

PRECEPT NINE: Resentment and complaining are not appropriate for the warrior or for anyone else.

PRECEPT TEN: Do not let yourself be guided by the feeling of lust or love.

PRECEPT ELEVEN: In all things, have no preferences.

PRECEPT TWELVE: Be indifferent to where you live.

PRECEPT THIRTEEN: Do not pursue the taste of good food.

PRECEPT FOURTEEN: Do not hold on to possessions you no longer need.

PRECEPT FIFTEEN: Do not act following customary beliefs.

PRECEPT SIXTEEN: Do not collect weapons or train with weapons beyond what is useful.

PRECEPT SEVENTEEN: Do not fear Death.

PRECEPT EIGHTEEN: Do not seek to either goods or fiefs for your old age.

PRECEPT NINETEEN: Respect Buddha and the Gods without counting on their help.

PRECEPT TWENTY: You may abandon your own body, but you must preserve your honor.

PRECEPT TWENTY-ONE: Never stray from the Way.

INTRODUCTION

"Man is bred for war..."
Frederick Nietzsche

For the last million or so years, our ancestors, both human and not-yet-human have been breeding under some very difficult conditions that required strength, speed, endurance, cunning and prowess. For the entirety of human existence, the ability to provide for ourselves and defend what is ours by force has been the most essential part of being alive[1].

You are the end product of generations of breeding designed to produce warriors. An engine fueled by passion selected for those traits that would make you strong and free. That engine was driven by a love of beauty and the desire to have families safe from tigers and disease and the warriors of other tribes.

Any virtue a man is capable of depends first on his prowess. It does not matter how loving a father you

---

[1] Today, that force is often outsourced to a government agency; a man in a uniform carrying a weapon who uses force on the state's behalf while pretending he serves you. For many of us, we no longer have to be strong and capable of effective violence, someone else can do that for us, after, of course, choosing what rights of ours they will preserve and which rights they will usurp. But I don't want you to imagine that, since the violence required to build and preserve is committed (or at least threatened) by some impersonal bureaucracy, it isn't still the foundation of every civilization whether you abide within the Empire of Nothing or outside its intent for you.

are, how talented a musician, how deep a thinker if you do not have a spear and the skill and strength to wield it when the adversary comes to make you a slave and make your woman his own.

You were bred to be good. You were bred to appreciate beauty and to foster it, to care for it; to love and laugh and be an instrument of joy to your tribe and your family. You were bred to enjoy the taste of a lover's kiss and the laughter of children.

But first you were bred to stand and fight and be a shield between those things and any adversary that might harm them.

You were bred for war.

There existed in Medieval Japan a warrior type known as the "ronin." A ronin was a member of his society's warrior caste, trained for war and expected to make his livelihood through his prowess, who somehow found himself outside the accepted military structures of his day.

I can think of no more fitting term for the veterans of the 21st century's War on Terror and for those men and women who study the martial arts seriously, aware that the life-giving sword is still a sword.

I am not going to downplay my opinion that every man is bred for war in a way that women are not. Nor am I going to downplay my complete approval of those women who now wear the blue cord of a US Army Infantryman and a Ranger tab in some instances. When women choose the Way of the Warrior they set themselves to overcome obstacles men do not encounter and that makes their success, therefore, in some ways even more glorious.

For the most part, veterans of previous wars found ways to leave their experiences behind them. Veterans of the Second World War came home from Europe and Asia and thought of their war as something they did. It left an impression, but, for the most part, it did not define them as they returned to civilian life to again become farmers and engineers. In no small part, this was because their war had involved the entire society for which they fought.

The Campaign in Korea quickly became known as The Forgotten War as it was wedged between the Great Crusade of World War Two and the debacle of Vietnam. These veterans, too, saw their war as something they did, but were the first American soldiers to be perceived as having not quite achieved victory and, despite their personal sacrifices and heroism, they returned to their civilian lives conscious that the civilian world had moved on without them.

Vietnam brought us a generation of veterans who were largely rejected by the civilian society they left behind. They were young men and their peers who had stayed home largely felt the war was not just imperfect but morally wrong and that the veteran accrued some guilt by his participation whether he was a volunteer or a draftee. Instead of being something he did, the Vietnam veteran experienced his war as something that happened to him, especially those men who were drafted and sought every chance of avoiding the war.

Rather than being assimilated back into the society he had served, the veteran found he must first reject the wars and its horrors and his own experience of suffering and heroism. (I don't mean to make this generalization sound universal. I've met more than a few veterans from the Vietnam War who, at 70 years old, still carry a certain amount of the bad-ass aura that a warfighter earns. And men in their 90's who remind you still of why the Nazi's never had a chance.)

This was the story every young man[2] who enlisted in the all-volunteer force that went to Iraq and Afghanistan was familiar with. We had seen the movies, THE DEER HUNTER, FIRST BLOOD, FULL METAL JACKET and BORN ON THE FOURTH OF JULY. We had been led to accept that war made men savages and broke their

---

[2] My editor (who is, by the way, an incredibly beautiful woman) made a note here saying, "I think somewhere here you need to explain that while women enlisted also, this work deals with the male experience." This never occurred to me because there is little I find stranger than women who write books about men. Christina Hoff-Sommers THE WAR AGAINST BOYS (Simon & Schuster 2000) being the only book about male experience written by a woman that I recommend. I think the experience of being a woman must be an infinitely complicated, intricate thing that I would fail to adequately address if I tried; the experience of the female veteran even more so. It might be fascinating to explore these precepts with a female infantryman and discover how much that experience of violence differs.

souls and such men were inevitably villains or merely pathetic.

The very act of enlisting into the military between 1975 and 2000 required a young man to first reject the civilian world he expected to reject him for his enlistment.

After the attacks of 11 September 2001, the civilian world divided itself into three factions based on how one saw the coming wars. One faction was eager to support the young soldier going forth to make the world safe and mete out justice to the adversary. Another faction rose up to protest, to again claim war was always wrong and that the warrior was always a psychotic murderer. A third faction tried to straddle the fence and "support the troops" but not support the war.

The soldiers I served with and have spoken to since had a nearly universal contempt for the last two factions. "Fuck those guys." And, rather than seek the approval of their peers who did not go forth into war, the soldier and the veteran mocked them. While previously veterans had accepted the idea their society rejected them and their peers held them in contempt as murderers, these veterans came to despise civilians as cowards and, unlike the previous generation of war veterans, it was never safe to spit on or mock them. They did not seek assimilation back into that faction of society that rejected them, they were willing to punch anyone who challenged their honor "right in the fucking throat."

Our Wars were neither "something we did" nor "something that happened to us" for the most part. Our wars became part of our identity and we remained warriors even upon our discharge.

I'm no expert on PTSD from the inside or out. In 2010, I underwent a court ordered psychiatric evaluation that established I had neither PTSD nor anger issues. While I still mourn the dead (some of whom died despite my best efforts to keep them alive), to do so is only natural and not a symptom of some "disorder." Achilles cried his eyes out when his cousin was killed by Hector.

I know PTSD is real. My grandmother's brother fought in Europe and, as a fascinated child who wanted to ask questions, I was cautioned not to mention it. He had "seen some things" and never discussed the War. He was a successful family man and his reluctance to speak of the war never manifested in any harmful way as far as I know.

But my first personal experience with the VA was an official talking to my squadron when we got home from Iraq telling us we could get a 30% disability rating simply for having a CMB, CIB or CAB[3]. It was, again, assumed that I was broken by my war.

---

[33] CMB=Combat Medic Badge, CIB=Combat Infantryman's Badge, CAB=Combat Action Badge. The CIB was created during WW2 for infantrymen who spent a certain amount of time in combat and, shortly after that, the CMB was created for medics who performed their job after being under fire with an infantry unit. The CAB came about when other career fields rightfully protested that they were getting shot at, too, and killing bad guys so they should get some

Since then, I have met a navy veteran who has a 70% disability rafting for her PTSD which, while she never went to Iraq or A-Stan, was a result of seeing body bags transferred to metal caskets in Qatar, and a veteran of my own squadron who tried to coach me on what lies to tell to get a disability check, and far too many clerks and IT guys who have PTSD because they witnessed mortar fire even though they never went outside the wire. Its my understanding, though I can't cite a source, that warfighters suffer PTSD at lower rates than those who stayed inside the wire.

In 1985 when I went to basic combat training, I was taught by my drill sergeants, some of whom were veterans of Vietnam, that I would one day die in the Fulda Gap or Nicaragua, but only after doing and seeing terrible things. I think that this aspect of my training inoculated me against PTSD to an extent. Knowing that war was horror and glory prepared me to face that unknown better than those young people who enlisted only after being assured that they'd never see combat and they'd be in a cozy air conditioned office in Baghdad or Kabul.

---

bling also. I used to say that the CIB and CAB were just "victims of violence" awards since you didn't have to do anything to earn them except be where a bad guy was getting rowdy, and to earn your CMB required you to treat the injured after being where a bad guy got rowdy. Then I started hearing about medics who were getting their CMB for making sure everyone was okay ("assessing a casualty" being part of the treatment of the wounded) after a mortar shell landed impotently within hearing distance.

The ugly truth is that there is a romance around PTSD. Again, we all know that ass clown who picks up girls by acting depressed and playing it off as what he saw during the war. There are some hippie chicks who LOVE that shit. And we all love hippie chicks.

This flippant attitude toward actual PTSD and the sickening glorification of "the 22 veterans who will commit suicide today" or the whining of that veteran who can't be around fireworks because it reminds him of artillery fire (which he never experienced from the receiving end) are the product, I think, of our society's devotion to weakness and vulnerability. The only way they can accept a display of that strength and prowess demonstrated by a 19 year old infantryman is to insist that he is somehow broken and even more vulnerable than they are.

And too many of my fellow veterans play along. I'm sure tyrants across the globe are glad to read on facebook that American soldiers are afraid of loud noises and our mothers all sleep more secure knowing their defenders can't distinguish between incoming fire and sparklers for emotional reasons.

I've had veterans act shocked when they learn I'm also a combat vet ("Have you ever killed anyone?" "A few that I know of...and a few more probably that I wasn't the only guy shooting at") but have no remorse for the killing I've done. That I can sit calmly and say "Everyone I ever killed needed to be dead" seems shocking to civilians and even to some veterans and definitely to inexperienced social workers new to the VA.

I'm tired of hearing the old aphorisms that those who did shit don't talk and those who talk didn't do shit. That might have been true in Vietnam but it seems every SEAL writes a book these days. I'm also tired of hearing that my assertion that war is glorious and it is no wonder men love it somehow demonstrates that I do not understand what war is. Especially when these protests come from men who paid ten bucks to see AMERICAN SNIPER (after shelling out $25 for the hardcover book) and SEAL TEAM has been renewed for a second season.

Anyway, once outside the accepted military system, we returned to combat as contractors, or started t-shirt companies (Article 15, Ranger UP, Grunt Style), coffee companies (Black Rifle Coffee Company), or forged a place in the fitness industry based on our military training. We continued to train in martial arts and with firearms, making videos for YouTube.

At least one veteran, Tim Kennedy, made a career as a Mixed Martial Artist, continuing to earn his livelihood with his understanding of violence. Many more of us, probably because we are not quite of Tim Kennedy's caliber, continue to sport fight and train simply because it is who we are.

There is even a TV network (VET TV) devoted to us and the understanding that our sense of humor is definitely not mainstream.

We are no longer soldiers, but we are still the most dangerous men in the room and we are still warriors.

Like the ronin, we are warriors without a place. Like the ronin, "our" society is uncertain what to make of us. The society we left behind still paints us as victims of our wars and laments the degree to which we suffer from PTSD while we laugh and talk about "that one time in Laghman Province...or Fallujah..."

In the days after the 11 September attacks, the military took in every man willing to fight. Regulations about tattoos and criminal backgrounds were revised. The vast majority of soldiers who came in during that time served with great honor and demonstrated that the nation's faith in them was justified. But as the wars drew to a close, the rules changed again and the war fighter often found himself without a place because of a juvenile possession charge or a tattoo on his neck.

Many of us are conscious of the fact that we are that segment of our society that is the most skilled at violence, the most fit, the most capable and that much of our society thinks we are meaningless or merely pay lip service to our prowess and our deeds (usually again tinged with pity.)

My own contempt for the system that created this society or the society that created this system has included the Army in a vague way. The politics and bullshit that are the day to day functioning of a peacetime army offends me. We were once warriors and our bodies and our minds and our machines were instruments with one purpose: to close with and kill the enemies of what is right and good. Now, vehicle gunnery is a skill secondary to one's ability to park that war machine online in the perfect 45 degree angle with every other vehicle. Go Cav.

Yet that contempt I feel has never spilled over into my feelings for the officers and men with which I served. They are too many to name here. They know who they are.

That said, I want to emphasize again that this volume was not written solely for the veterans of my wars. Frederick Nietzsche wrote, "Every man is bred for war." Every man is the descendant of a man who looked up from his fire at a passing mammoth and said, "I'm gonna go stab that thing with a sharp stick. Then we'll eat like kings." His friends laughed, said he was crazy, and then said, "Wait a minute. I'll come with you."

The timid have no descendants among us.

In this volume, I refer to what Guillaume Faye writes of as THE CONVERGENCE OF CATASTROPHES[4] and to what Jack Donovan calls "the Empire of Nothing.[5]" Much of the weakness prevalent in our society are, I think, a direct result of the rejection of the warrior aspect of the human psyche.

---

[4]CONVERGENCE OF CATASTROPHES by Guillaume Faye, Arktos Media Ltd. 2012
[5] BECOMING A BARBARIAN by Jack Donovan, Dissonant Hum, 2016 (also read THE WAY OF MEN and SKY WITHOUT EAGLES by the same author)

Men have become reluctant to assert strength and dominance, instead being forced to question whether masculinity is inherently "toxic." In the name of prudence and security, men are urged (and sometimes forced) to turn over the responsibility for their own safety to the state. Loud political voices tell us again and again that it is just "common sense" that no man should possess a weapon.

Politicians see a world where catastrophic acts of violence end the lives of scores at churches and schools and concerts and the well lit streets of our biggest, most well protected cities. Their answer is to demand men make themselves more helpless and seek greater dependence on police departments and systems that are already over taxed and failing. I don't understand this.

I worry that their only sincere ambition is to base the eternal increase of their power on that dependence. I worry that their intent is simply our submission. Mostly I worry because it simply isn't possible for the ronin not to be dangerous when what he loves is threatened.

This weakness and the worship of vulnerability is only one of the looming catastrophes. The climate, the economy, the rising tides of extremism of all sorts, the obesity epidemic, the inevitable depletion of the world's oil supply, the even more critical poisoning of the world's water supply all serve to bring the world entire closer to some brink past which the Empire will not survive and neither will those dependent on it.

This volume is for every man who sees these deeds as provocation and who decides that he will stand for the safety of his family and that his own strength must be sufficient in times of crisis. Even if he must stand alone. Especially if he must stand alone. A ronin.

Miyamoto Musashi was also a ronin, a wandering samurai without a master. A week before his death, he wrote the DOKKODO for one of his pupils. It is not a treatise on swordsmanship like his more famous work GO RIN NO SHO (THE BOOK OF FIVE RINGS), but a simple letter about the life of a ronin. It is 21 simple precepts and Musashi left behind no commentary, though he probably discussed these precepts at length with his student.

Musashi was an extreme individual and it is difficult to adopt and discuss his teachings without seeming to be equally extreme. I am certain I have failed in this regard. In discussing Musashi's Thirteenth Precept ("Do Not Pursue The Taste Of Good Food"), I understand his position and I agree wholeheartedly. But I cannot betray the sincerity of my relationship with tacos. That dedication outstrips even my dedication to jujitsu on some Tuesday nights.

Is this hypocrisy?

Perhaps it is.

But I am not a ronin making his warrior's pilgrimage across medieval Japan. I am a warrior without a lord, a man whose sword is his own and has no formal obligation to any other. My devotion to the Way is not the pure intent of a saint or a Buddha.

There is a paradox that my devotion is to prowess for the sake of prowess, but that prowess then exists for the sake of what it defends and what it guards; the laughter of children, the taste of caramel, the way a woman walks when she knows a man is watching.

Musashi isn't exempt from this judgement either. While claiming to "Walk The Way Alone" he had his students and his admirers, much as you and I have our friends and family and our students. He proscribes us from seeking fiefs and laurels, but he applied more than once to be accepted by a Daimyo.

In a sense, every man walks The Way Alone. How each man defines "alone" may vary. Some will be more truly alone than Musashi was, without friends or family or cause. Others will have friends and sons at their flanks, but recognize that they have no one to rely on or defer to when it comes time to act.

When I comment on the Way Alone, I'm referring most to the fact that only the man himself can determine how hard he will train, how seriously he takes his role as a warrior. You are completely alone inside your own psyche, exercising your own will, in the gym and on the dojo floor and on every path your foot sets out upon.

You are alone when you stand outside the will of consumerism and what the empire's corporate masters intend for you.

But it is also necessary, I think, to consider Musashi and these precepts in the most extreme interpretation possible, because that is what the world will look like when it is time to confront the adversary in that life and death and struggle. In that moment when you are fighting for all that matters, the most extreme interpretation of "alone" will be the focus of your experience. Since you will fight as you train, drawing close to these extremes, at least from time to time, is an essential part of the ronin experience.

And that is how I presented them here. Devoid in places of humor and joy, this commentary passes over many of the lighter aspects of life that actually give our prowess and our devotion to the way meaning.

This small volume is my understanding of The Way of Walking Alone.

Precept One: Accept Things Exactly As They Are

The world is a dangerous place.

Confusion makes it a more dangerous place.

This essay is the longest in this book because this precept is the foundation of everything that comes after. While it is inevitable that we are all going to be mistaken about aspects of our world and our lives, any voluntary willingness to live a lie we know to be a lie is a form of suicide. Any authentic life, whether as a warrior or as a shopkeeper begins with an attempt to discern the truth and live within its bounds even as we struggle to stretch those bounds and make the world more to our liking.

In the perfect world as I envision it, every man, regardless of his profession and his status, would see himself first and foremost as a warrior/poet/scholar. The cornerstones of a man's life should be prowess and strength, love and beauty, wisdom and knowledge. That's the world as I think it should be.

I do not let my hopes and my desires push aside my awareness that this is not the world as it is. If I cannot accept the world as it is, then I have zero chance of coaxing it toward being as I think it should be.

This is the most vital point of this most vital precept, perhaps. Like the Stoic admonition to not concern ourselves with things outside our control[6], it is

---

[6] DISCOURSES by Epictetus I.1 "We must make the best of those things that are in our power, and take the rest as nature gives it."

often misunderstood as advocating resignation rather than resiliency. Am I to accept Racism? Terrorism? Corrupt judges? The designs of evil men who intend to take my life?

Of course not. There are many things that must be resisted and fought against. But before you can fight against racism or poverty or social injustice in any form, you must understand it and you must accept it exactly as it is.

Only by an accurate understanding of how any given situation "really is" can you find that weak point where it can be toppled. For example, the best opposition to racism is understanding and experience.

By working together, playing together, and sharing our lives with people of different ethnicities, religions, and creeds, we can learn how to live together with respect and compassion. We can attempt understanding. We can find that place where good men of every race can stand together and say, "Those other guys are assholes" based solely on the content of those assholes's character.

Encouraging black athletes not to go to "white" universities doesn't achieve anything other than to make a faction of the professional victim's guild feel warm fuzzies about their own issues and hatreds.

"Accepting reality as it is" doesn't mean we are impotent and that injustice or unfortunate situations must be tolerated merely because they are "the way things are." One aspect of every such situation is the degree to which it can be changed and the methods required to bring about that change.

One aspect of reality that must be accepted is that complaint alone seldom accomplishes anything. Those deluded fools who run their mouths and condemn verbally, imagining that their protest has meaning and might alone bring change accomplish nothing but seem well satisfied with themselves.

One problem the West has had confronting Islamic Terrorism in particular is a refusal to accept it for what it is. There are scholars who argue ceaselessly that the root of this terror is economic; if the terrorists only had jobs and better economic prospects, they'd be less willing to be suicide bombers. Maybe if they had real freedom. President Bush said they hate us because we are free. Bill Maher said they hate us because we don't know why they hate us.

And these positions then become the stages on which Islamic Terrorism is confronted with an astonishing lack of success. The terrorists themselves claim they are fighting us and hate us because they are ordered to do so by God. They hate us and make war against us because we are not Muslims or, at least, not the same sort of Muslims they are.

But this assertion is labeled as "Islamaphobia" and racism by academics who have given up belief in Gods and Crusades and Jihads long ago. Having no fanatical faith in a god and an afterlife, they fail to understand and respond to those who do.[7]

---

[7] Time to play the "some of my best friends" card. I deployed to

Accepting the uncomfortable truth that our enemy is motivated by faith and a desire for martyrdom could help us find that strategy that brings some sort of victory. Continuing to plan strategy around ideas that have been proven to be false can not bring peace.

This problem is made worse because in today's political atmosphere, neither side is listening. It seems impossible for two men to disagree and argue. Usually when I have said to a leftist, "I think you're wrong and this is why..." I am answered with, "Then you're an intolerant bigot who should be punched in the face." The same thing happens when I argue with those on the right, except there I'm called a "liberal sheep" by some idiot who came no closer to the war than a strongly worded Facebook post.

Neither side is interested enough in "things exactly as they are" if there is the slightest possibility this understanding and acceptance would disrupt the fantasy that their "side" is pushing forward as an agenda. As a result, the Afghan War has become the longest and most expensive in US History. I do not speak as a citizen interested in politics (I'm really not) but as a

---

Iraq and Afghanistan with Muslims who were loyal to their faith and to the United States. In Afghanistan, I took my meals with the Afghans at every opportunity because I enjoyed their company and they had better food. I am in no way hostile to al-Islam. But I'm also not afraid to provoke and upset violent fanatics of any faith (or none). This "jihad" is aimed at my friends and my children, so its adherents will be extinguished. And al-Islam will be better for their extinction.

soldier who sought to win and defend what I cherish by ending the threat to it.

This tendency to reject or ignore the reality of "things exactly as they are" is distressingly widespread. In the past several years, I've heard again and again that expecting people to act in accord with the way things are is either "victim blaming" or simply heartless cruelty.

After the school shootings on 14 Feb 2018 in Florida, a new call went out to ban "assault rifles" and, in many circles, all firearms. In the minds of many on the political left, it is simply impossible to trust anyone outside the service of the state with a weapon.[8] If you're reading this, you probably already know the statistics that demonstrate this assertion is absurd and have had to more than once assert that the right to bear arms is rooted in the Founders's unwillingness to trust the state with the preservation of life, liberty, and the pursuit of happiness[9].

---

[8] This example shows the insanity of this faction that desires to be helpless. Their protests are contradictory and nonsensical. "The Current President is worse than Hitler, only he should have guns." "The police hunt and murder young men of color, only they should have guns!"

[9] While everyone wants to point at the second amendment, I like to point at Article I, Section 8 of the US Constitution which explains that Congress will have the power to grant Letters of Marque and Reprisal. It was assumed that there would be times when private citizens led naval and militia forces so powerful that the government might want to borrow them.

But imagine for a moment, and this isn't that difficult, that their political agenda is going to succeed; all firearms will be banned in the United States at some point. Will it be six months? Five years? Ten?

Until then...what will they do?

No matter how ardently we all wish for a community of loving siblings, no matter how certain some might be that ridding civilians of firearms is a cornerstone of this future utopia, between now and then, how do they intend to survive this dangerous gun-filled world?

It seems that when there are shootings, many sincere people who sympathize with the victims post on social media that their "thoughts and prayers" are with the victims. And more and more, those who advocate against being armed proclaim that thoughts and prayers are simply not enough.

But if you refuse to arm yourself in a world where evil men are armed, if you refuse to train in a world where evil men are willing to act, if you trust your security completely to the state, what are you really relying on besides hope and prayer?

Any understanding of the world that concedes there are dangerous armed villains out there who mean to harm the innocent, and that you and your family may find yourself in their company, has to include either a fatalistic acceptance of suffering and death or a desire to defend yourself and everything you cherish with whatever force the situation requires.

Knowing the adversary waits for us in the dark corners of every situation and place where he sees an opportunity, how can any of us suggest that we are made safer by being fat, slow, weak, untrained, and disarmed?

Of course, expecting people to take a measure of responsibility for their own safety is also unacceptable to many. Something in the current mindset, this sense of "entitlement" that goes back much further than the "millennials" insists that it be kept from harm as a matter of course despite their own decisions. To question their poor decisions is "victim blaming."

In May 2017, Nolan Bruner was sentenced to four months for a sexual assault. It's easy to agree that this absurd sentence should have been much greater for the crime of rape. But the lesson here that might actually benefit women is taboo to even discuss.

His victim went to a party where she knew no one and there indulged in drugs with a man she did not know even AFTER he asked her for sex.[10]

To suggest that she should have not done these things, to suggest that she bears even the slightest responsibility for how her conduct and her decisions impacted what happened to her is itself criminal in the eyes of those who benefit from an agenda furthered by her victimization.

---

[10] Pay attention to this part, ladies, and carry away this one lesson: If a man asks you for sex, and you refuse, but he hangs around anyway: he is far too beta for you to waste your company on OR HE HAS ILL INTENT. Every fucking time.

She was not only a victim to Nolan Bruner's lust, but she was a sacrifice to that agenda and so is every girl and woman taught that she has no obligation to accept the reality that her safety is her own responsibility more than any other's. Even today when this topic is discussed with many people, the reality that what she did was stupid and contributed to her assault is rejected.

As I listen to a generation of women and their "beta" male allies fed on the promises and assertions of "whatever wave" feminism, who then find themselves victimized or witnesses to another's victimization, I hear again and again that the world "should be" a certain way. Men "should be" different. A woman "should be" able to dance naked at the club, blackout drunk, and never be molested.

I agree completely. That is how things "should be." But the reality is that when a woman does those things, bad things are likely to happen. Rejecting the reality that bad things happen does not protect our young feminist.

When a woman goes to a club or frat party where she knows no one and gets black-out drunk, she is relying on reality "as it should be" and refusing to accept things as they are. Is her subsequent rape her own fault? Of course not.

But it is important also to acknowledge that she made poor choices and that poor choices almost always lead to disaster. To assert the truth that her rapist is solely responsible for his own decisions to commit atrocity doesn't save her NOR does it provide a lesson that might save her sisters.

Instead, we continue to see stories of "victims" who seem to have consciously rejected the idea that they are responsible to any degree for their own safety. Replacing an accurate understanding of the obvious dangerous in a situation with wishful thinking and a self-righteous assertion that every situation "should be" safe, these victims take ridiculous chances and then are genuinely surprised when bad things happen.

Whether it is appropriate or not to blame some toxic aspect of masculinity itself for the deeds of some men, such blame would do NOTHING to protect the young feminist and NOTHING to prevent such occurrences in the future. That blame only serves to use the victim's pain as a political tool.

Nothing is gained by screaming, "Teach Boys Not To Rape!" at rallies where strong, smart, independent adults wear hats shaped like vaginas.[11] You have no control over the actions of others. You have complete control over your own decisions. The first step, but by no means the final answer, is to accept these things exactly as they are. THEN prepare to confront and resist.

---

[11] And fucking get over this idea that THIS is a rape culture and that boys aren't taught "not to rape." You want a generation of angry young criminals? Teach them that their basic instincts are criminal. This idiotic assertion that every male is a born rapist is a strategy designed to deny reality, force a worldview in its place that serves a political end, but that will accomplish nothing.

Accepting reality exactly as it is might protect that young feminist from such crimes by giving her an understanding of how to avoid them. I question the motives of everyone who wants to shut that conversation down.

That this glorification of the victim then encourages false reporting is another fact that has to be accounted for in the minds of those who seek to reject "things as they are." When Aziz Ansari doesn't call a woman after a date and is then falsely accused of raping her, we're expected to struggle to understand how she "felt violated." When another false accuser wears a mattress on her back for years as a piece of performance art that ruins a young man's life, we're expected to wrestle with the idea that in some fashion her lie is really representative of a greater truth.

These are the mental gymnastics that come so easily to those who refuse to accept things as they really are.

Following Musashi's recommendation (and the recommendation of so many others in every time and place) I try to live in the world "as it is" while struggling to bring us all closer to the world "as I think it should be". This is the obligation of the warrior, I think. This is the Dharma of the Kshatriya, the Way of the Samurai who truly intends to wield a life-giving sword.

In the military and in law enforcement, we refer often to "situational awareness", the constant vigilance intended to keep us alert to nuances in the environment in order to enable us to respond appropriately if a threat presents itself. It requires the individual to comprehend the significance of variables, such as the dress and demeanor of people in the area, the availability of improvised weapons, terrain and even weather. This comprehension then allows the warrior to make appropriate estimations of threat, danger and how best to respond.

Misunderstanding of a situation can only lead to one of two errors: perceiving a threat where there is none or failing to perceive a threat where one is present. Having better situational awareness than your adversary makes you aware of threats that he might prefer were hidden and even leave him unaware that you are alert to the reality of your situation. Acting when there is no genuine threat exposes you to just retaliation and makes you the villain, no matter how sincere your fear.

Remaining unaware of threats means, of course, that when mere threat becomes actual attack or danger, your response to that danger will be based on a sudden appearance and not a careful evaluation. You will respond slower and you may respond with much less force than the situation demands or, possibly, much more force. It is also possible you will be incapacitated suddenly and finally by a threat you never saw coming.

Taking personal responsibility and accepting that one has a duty to maintain their own situational awareness requires that you willingly work within the reality that the world can be dangerous and that your assertions about how the world "should be" are meaningless when confronted by the way the world actually is.

Musashi exhorted his pupil to accept reality. The Modern Age exhorts us to refuse to accept reality and insist again and again on the "way things should be", hoping that such stubborn insistence alone will create a new reality.

Such an attitude can only led to more victims.

It is the warrior's responsibility to study and understand the world through which he moves. Before deploying to Iraq and Afghanistan, we were given classes on the worldview of the culture we were about to be immersed in. It wasn't necessary that we agree. It wasn't necessary that we adopt. It was necessary that we accept.

The most well-known example of such a cultural more is that residents of Iraq and A-Stan and much of the rest of the Middle East do nothing with their left hand. You and I might think it silly. We might think the reason for this habit is absurd. That doesn't matter. If you want to get along with these people and secure their co-operation, you have to accept that they think WE are the ones lacking culture because we differ from them.

Those who marched in and insisted that "we are the Americans and will do as we please" without regard for our ally's perception of the world were rejecting this reality; imagining they could force their understanding on their environment and refusing to instead work with the situation as it really was. Whether we were foolish to use paper instead of hand or not, we looked foolish to our allies and many of us never understood that.

Sun Tzu advised us that we must understand terrain, our enemy and our self. Only a fool would insist that his army can advance into Russia and not accept the reality of weather. Only a fool would look at the lessons of the colonial wars and every war since and suggest that technology is ever a good substitute for a simple willingness to fight.

And only a fool fails to understand that getting old and fat make you less dangerous than you were at twenty.

Yet we find ourselves surrounded by men who refuse to accept that reality exactly as it is: men who are certain they can handle a gun though they haven't been to the range in years, men who are certain they have what it takes to kill without remorse despite the evidence of 22 veteran suicides a day that suggest such things are more complicated than they appear sitting in your armchair.

Denial of this reality exactly as it is and the failure to counter and slow the degenerative effects of age by remaining focused on fitness and training is the exact same sort of mistake we discussed above. That man who ignores his fitness level and carries a handgun that he does not train with is possibly a greater fool than the young woman taking the wrong risks at a college party.

The warrior doesn't have time to waste confronting fantasy or making excuses. He doesn't wish his enemy were a better man who had no vices and sought only peace. (Well, he might, but he doesn't rely on that hope.) He understands that all efforts at diplomacy must be rooted in the reality of present enmity and accompanied by a willingness to destroy rather than become extinct himself.

He doesn't wish his terrain were easier and his allies identical to him. He packs light, he packs warm, and he smiles when his allies need to see him smile. He doesn't think a new M4 and body armor, stockpiles of food and ammo, and a weekend camping with his disorganized militia constitutes actual preparedness. He lifts, he runs, he cares for the only two weapons that matter: his mind and his body.

Accept things exactly as they are. The only thing you can change and determine the course of is your own decision making. Unpleasant realities cannot be avoided by mere denial.

But if you study a situation and explore the conditions that create and perpetuate it, accepting everything you find exactly as it is, you might find where one can push and bring the whole thing down. Or at least weaken it so it is less unpleasant and less dangerous.

Lastly, we must also accept the reality that we will not always understand completely. That sometimes facts and information are sketchy and we must proceed anyway. One reality we must always accept is that no plan survives contact with the adversary and you will often learn only by being confronted by your misunderstandings.

Everything in these precepts and this commentary comes back to this: Accept things exactly as they are.

Precept Two: Do Not Seek Pleasure For Its Own Sake

When Musashi wrote these precepts, he wasn't writing for all of us. He wasn't writing for you and me. He was writing for one student; Terao Magonojo. He wasn't writing for shopkeepers who attend a martial arts class twice a week. He was writing for a student who would face death every time he drew his weapon and was depending on that "Way" as his path to enlightenment and salvation. Unlike his previous work, it may be that Musashi had no intention of this letter becoming part of his canon.

Every warrior understands that prowess is part of the key to survival. When confronted by those who intend to destroy you or what you love, you must have the strength and skill to overcome their strength and skill. But for Musashi, and those samurai like him who considered the sword a vehicle to enlightenment, prowess is part of the path to salvation.

If you study a martial art that ends in -do (Aikido, Judo, Karatedo, Hwarang-Do) then you should understand already that "-do" means "Way" in the exact same manner that "Dharma" means "Way". When Musashi says "the Way" he is referring to this concept. The Way of the Sword. The Way of Walking Alone.

That said, perhaps it is important to ask whether every man has a duty as a warrior to train and study and think upon these things as though he, too, were facing extinction at every moment. Perhaps our shopkeeper needs to keep death in his mind at all times, prepared for the robber who lies in wait when he locks his shop at night. Then again, perhaps he is not committed to -do as a path to enlightenment or salvation.

The Hindus believed that each caste had its own Dharma. What was good and proper for the Brahmin might not be good and proper for the Ksatriya and might not be good and proper for the shopkeeper. What is good and proper for our shopkeeper attending a taekwondo class twice a week to keep fit might not be what is good and proper for another shopkeeper who attends the same class because he lives in a violent neighborhood alone with his elderly mother.

Musashi is writing these precepts for a man who will study the sword and train because his life depends on it. The ronin accepts that at every moment, even when drunk at a geisha house, he is possibly only moments away from a fight for his life.

Also, just as that rabbi said, "If you can't leave everything else behind, don't try to follow me[12]," Musashi would caution that if you're not following this path with singleminded devotion, its probably better not to lift a sword at all. Its certainly safer.

It is that warrior, not the hobbyist, that Musashi cautions, "Do not seek pleasure for its own sake" but note that Musashi does not say, "Do not seek pleasure." He says do not seek pleasure "for its own sake."

And so we must seek to distinguish the two.

---

[12] Luke Chapter 14 paraphrased by the author.

As a warrior, even a warrior who spends the majority of his time as a shopkeeper or a doctor or a carpenter, it is necessary to put training and fighting ahead of everything else. Those two arenas must occupy all of our time. By fighting, I don't necessarily mean a physical struggle. Sitting here at this laptop writing these words is fighting. Reading about how better to push my ideas into the world is training.

It is probable, and certainly to be hoped, that many devoted warriors will never actually have to defend what they love. But the way is in training, and being prepared for a life and death struggle is necessary if you intend to preserve what you hold dear on that random occasion you meet an adversary who will kill to suppress what you think is Good.

So, if we lift for two hours a day, and train jujitsu and boxing for two hours a day and have 40 hour a week jobs, that leaves about 72 hours a week for study and recreation. We have families, children, who are owed far more time than we seem to have to give them.

My point isn't that our lives are too busy to train. You're a warrior, training should be a given, sleep and work might be optional. My point is that we have SO much time for recreation that we need to ask whether we are using that time as we should or whether we are merely killing time by seeking pleasure for its own sake. Especially on those days we skip the gym or the training mat.

The Stoic Philosopher Seneca wrote, "It is not that we have a short space of time, but that we waste much of it. Life is long enough, and it has been given in sufficiently generous measure to allow the accomplishment of the very greatest things if the whole of it is well invested.[13]"

Training and constant vigilance require energy. There's nothing wrong with recharging your batteries by playing guitar and drinking a few beers with your brothers. There's nothing wrong with eating delicious food (a precept we will encounter later). There's nothing wrong with sitting for hours in a room lit only by the TV watching a show with your fingers in your wife's hair allowing your day and hers to end pleasantly.

We must, however, never allow these activities to become a reason unto themselves. We will never have so much time that it can be wasted simply distracting ourselves from ourselves.

When I get a pizza and sit alone in the back of my truck, eating too many carbs and undoing the work accomplished that morning at the gym, I am indulging in pleasure for the sake of pleasure. When I take my youngest son to Chuck E Cheese and eat an even less healthy pizza (and drink soda) the purpose of our pleasure is bonding over video games and the accumulation of tickets to be exchanged for plunder. It is, in effect, training time for two warriors as we throw skee-balls and gun down aliens.

---

[13] ON THE SHORTNESS OF LIFE by Lucius Seneca (translated by Gareth Williams) available online at:
https://archive.org/stream/SenecaOnTheShortnessOfLife/Seneca+on+the+Shortness+of+Life_djvu.txt

No form of recreation...provided it doesn't undo your training...is unhealthy or unnecessary provided it is done always with an eye toward your role as a warrior.

I play Dungeons and Dragons with my sons. We play Minecraft on XBox. There are few activities that I would condemn out of hand as never having any benefit. Smoking, perhaps. The use of dangerous recreational drugs. This precept only condemns those pleasures that claim our time and our strength and benefit no one. And we are surrounded by such pleasing vices in this age.

Much of a warrior's pleasure comes not through a dedicated seeking but from his ability to take his pleasure where he finds it. You cannot seek the sunset or the sunrise or the love of a beautiful woman. Such things come to you as result of living your life according to a certain way.

The Pick-up Artist, a phenomenon much more written of several years ago and now evolved into the "Red Pill" and "MGTOW[14]" movements, was a

---

[14] The MGTOW movement is a fascinating study. One of the tropes of the PUA community is that women prefer "jerks" to "nice guys." For this reason, the PUA seeks to be seen as a minor league jerk, still lovable, but a little too strong and self confident to be bullied by women, instead being the one to playfully bully them and the other girls they know flock to his alpha persona. MGTOW (Men Going Their Own Way) take this idea to the extreme that they reject the idea of any permanent relationship with a woman and, in so many words, despise women and abandon any intention of having their company for any purpose beyond sexual relief. And I think most of them are lying about getting that.

commitment to pleasure. By closely observing the behavior of women, these men reconstructed their identity and adopted traits that they perceived as defining the "Alpha," that man among men found irresistible by women. Their primary goal seemed, to me, to be some validation of their worth that had its root in the approval and desire of these women.

This collection of skills and attributes was called "Game." Though it is intensely denied now, calling it "Game" was perfect because it involved a very deep pretense. To women, the PUA asserts, it doesn't matter whether you are strong and brave and a leader; it only matters that you are perceived so[15]. Accepting reality is rejected if that reality doesn't bring you a woman's attention. Allowing reality to guide a woman's decision whether to climb in bed with you or not was especially undesirable.

The Red Pill Man asserts instead that the only reality that matters is the reality defined by female thought patterns (and, paradoxically, the approval and desire women have for men who impose their own thought patterns.) My assertion that a man should be strong and brave because battle is always imminent is far less valuable to them than the assertion that a man

---

[15] One uncomfortable reality is that such perception is vital to many people in many fields. There is a certain amount of truth in an assertion that what you appear to be can be more important than what you really are in a world that rejects a commitment to truth or when engaged in a task that requires deceiving others. "When weak appear strong; when strong appear weak" is not useless advice.

must be well built to attract female attention and appear brave when it is not too dangerous to do so.

To that pick-up artist, the worth of any attribute is measured solely by the application it has to claiming the pleasure of a woman's company. That they are committed to a lie is evidenced by their own lamentation that so man great PUAs eventually wreck themselves when they meet a girl that they are so enamored of that they find themselves unable to maintain the pretense. These stories are given as lessons in the literature of the PUA and the Red Pill man that one must never allow his genuine affection for a girl to lead him to be too open and honest with her.

As the warrior pursues the Way, he accepts reality and confronts it and changes as experience forces him to and the situation demands, but, I think, he holds close to his unalterable identity as a warrior (and often his identity as a husband and father, also) seeking a more intimate relationship with reality because his very life and the existence of all he defends depends on it. He refuses to live a lie, insisting that he partake only in sincere, honest relationships.

Perhaps the way of the PUA is a "Way" as well. But, if so, it is a Way that posits everything real can be sacrificed for one's own pleasure.

The first popular book about the Pick Up Artist community was Neil Strauss's THE GAME[16]. The book ends on an almost tragic note as the author finds that Game has become a thing of ridicule among the women

---

[16] THE GAME by Neil Strauss, Reganbooks, 2005

he targets, as they have seen through it. His mentor and guide has wrecked himself on the rock of a woman for whom he has dropped his game, seeking, one supposes, to be loved for what he is rather than for what he struggles so hard to appear to be.

In our dedication to the idea that we must accept reality exactly as it is, we must be especially committed to knowing and understanding ourselves. Then we must live that truth to avoid the symbolic suicide that comes when we repress our identity and live a part designed to please another.

Among many of those who study and write about men, there is also much attention and worry, too, about pornography and masturbation, a concern that should draw laughter from every soldier who ever had to tend to his own pleasure in places far removed from the company of available women. Most of us masturbated and looked at porn the way men back at home, well, masturbated and looked at porn.

For us, however, it wasn't pleasure for its own sake so much as that necessary relief and escape from the environment we were in. Where there were women, we pursued them. Where there were not, we fantasized.

Here in the real world, however, studies have demonstrated than men are developing bizarre aberrations tied to porn consumption. Consuming this pleasure for its own sake, in lieu of actual intimacy with a woman (or simply sex), has had a negative impact on their social interactions and their self-image.

My point isn't that masturbation and porn are bad, even though I do have my own prudish concerns about porn. It's that masturbation is, in most instances, the epitome of pleasure for the sake of pleasure and it is NOT without physical and psychological consequence for the warrior[17].

Except in extreme circumstances such as experienced in small outposts in Afghanistan, it's always better to pursue women[18] and actual physical

---

[17] I originally intended to write an appendix or two about porn, masturbation, intermittent fasting and meditation. It'd be another book. Instead, I want to send you off to look this stuff up on your own. On the subject of porn and masturbation: https://youtu.be/wSF82AwSDiU In short, you don't have to get fully erect when masturbating and your brain starts working with that lower physical standard. And what kind of beta gets off on watching other men fuck instead of going out and fucking himself? Well, not fucking himself; that'd just be masturbation. You know what I mean. Further, there seems too be some negative impact on testosterone production if you masturbate versus having actual sex. This research is controversial and I have to admit I don't understand much of it. On intermittent fasting: https://youtu.be/4UkZAwKoCP8 In short, fasting is good for you. That's why every religion recommends it. Intermittent fasting can be part of the Keto diet and was researched largely thanks to the benefit it renders people with epilepsy. Meditation: https://youtu.be/m8rRzTtP7Tc I picked some quick TED talks as a starting point. You'll find what interests you, hopefully, what adds to your practice of the Way and go from there. On cold showers: https://youtu.be/GShvGXwaijg For me, the most important part of a cold shower is that it is terribly uncomfortable and therefore a real practice in facing discomfort and an exercise in will.
[18] Okay, it doesn't have to be women. I don't care who you're exploring intimacy with. (My editor, who is a beautiful woman

relationships that add to our lives and inspire us than to simply stroke our cocks while watching other men fuck our favorite porn starlets.

This, then, becomes the vital point for the ronin in the 21st Century: pleasure and recreation must be seen in the context of furthering your aims as a warrior whether those aims are that you support and defend your family or the perfection of prowess for its own sake. If it does not increase the harmony you feel within and without, it must be cast away no matter how good it feels.

For my own part, I struggle with this precept constantly. I want Pepsi and tacos, that aforementioned pizza, and a little time alone with Lexi Belle. Like too many Americans, I have to struggle so that what should be an occasional indulgence in pleasure does not threaten to become a daily indulgence.

I recently examined my life, the amount of time I wasted when I should be training or fighting and made the decision to live outdoors. I have been able to put more money into my business ideas, have been more diligent about training and nutrition, but best of all, I have rediscovered the pleasure of waking up to the sky after a night spent falling asleep under the stars.

I have an infinite access to pleasures...but none of them exist for their own sake now. It becomes obvious to me now that the pleasure I chase for its own sake is always a vice.

---

discouraged me from using the "F" word again.)

If you recognize that you have pleasures that you cannot discard even though they hold you back, you have to examine whether these addictions are such that you willingly step away from the Way of Walking Alone. There will be legions who cannot follow this Dharma, this Do, this Way because they cannot set aside a thing they find pleasurable even though it weakens them in some way.

Precept Three: Do Not Ever Rely On A Partial Feeling

In THE COMPLEAT GENTLEMAN[19], Brad Miner tells us that a gentleman should hold his own beliefs, his own code, so dear that when the time comes to give his life for what he believes, it should appear he cast his life away as though it meant nothing to him. That is how action appears when one depends on a belief that is complete, whole. One can put everything one is into that action and proceed without hesitation.

This isn't always possible. Not every belief we hold is so complete, so whole that we can act on it so decisively.

Is Musashi advising us to only act when you're absolutely certain of your reasons, the environment, the adversary, the desired outcome? This would be impossible and would leave us trapped in inaction while we constantly gathered new information and re-examined our beliefs.

What Musashi is advising us here is that one can rely on and act so decisively only on whole feelings, despite incomplete information. If we are not certain enough of our cause that we would die and "cast away our life as though it meant nothing" then our sword should stay in its scabbard. Our commitments, especially those values and people we have decided we

---

[19] THE COMPLEAT GENTLEMAN by Brad Milner, Spence Publishing, 2004

would accept extinction for, must be based on a mingling of reason and passion that can only evolve when we have thoroughly explored our selves and the object and identified then answered all of our own questions and concerns.

If we are required to act on partial feelings, information, and commitments we recognize are imperfect and incomplete, we must not depend on the course such feeling would insist on without being prepared to alter that course when we learn the feeling or incomplete belief we are acting on is wrong. There is little in life more difficult than admitting we are wrong. Making that admission, even to ourselves, in the middle of action is even more difficult. But that is exactly what is required when we strive to accept everything exactly as it is.

When considering this precept, it's important to keep in mind the idea that any "partial feeling" must also include contamination by its opposite. A partial feeling that a man is trustworthy admits to a partial feeling that the same man is not trustworthy. Neither of those feelings can then possibly be relied upon.

I, personally, have many times watched the failure of my plans and thought, "I saw that coming" or "I knew..." or better, "I should have known..." This is the after effect of relying on a partial feeling. When we are genuinely mistaken, failure comes as a surprise.

Following this precept then requires that we take upon ourselves two habits. First, we must examine our beliefs closely. We must know what we believe utterly (and hope it reflects the first precept's admonishment to accept things exactly as they are) and what beliefs we cannot commit to wholly. An incomplete belief, whether moral or concerning the nature of things, need not be abandoned, but it must be recognized as only partial.

This dictum is one of the core teachings of Sun Tzu's ART OF WAR[20]. In it, he warns that, "If you know the enemy and know yourself, you need not fear the result of a hundred battles. If you know yourself but not the enemy, for every victory gained you will also suffer a defeat. If you know neither the enemy nor yourself, you will succumb in every battle." What you know is key to victory in life and battle. This includes having a solid command of what Dick Cheney called "the known unknowns" in your own life and situation.

The ego often gets involved in this process. Many of us are far more likely to viciously defend a belief we are only half committed to than to admit that degree of uncertainty in our lives. We might then find ourselves following a path laid out by some assertion that we are unconvinced of but unwilling to humbly admit even the possibility of error.

I have a pretty solid conviction that the US Constitution is the most perfect political document. It is only "pretty solid" and not "absolute" because I do not

---

[20] THE ART OF WAR by Sun Tzu, Oxford University Press, 1963. (There are many good editions out there by many translators and publishers. I use this one because I wanted the introduction by B.H. Liddell-Hart.)

know the details of most other governments (I am not terribly interested in political theory) and because the romantic in me wants a monarchy while the rebel in me wants anarchy. I also recognize that the constitution hasn't been a meaningful part of how our government works for over a hundred years.

My decision to enlist in 1985 was not fueled by patriotism. Enlistment is one of those "all or nothing" decisions a man makes in his life. You place yourself entirely in the hands of a system that openly admits it will risk or spend your life as it sees fit and expect you to obey. Doing so on the basis of a partial feeling of patriotism would be foolish.

I enlisted because I wanted to know the things soldiers know. I wanted the skill set that comes with being an infantryman in an army. I had no doubts about this. Had I been born in any other country, I would have still found myself in the army.

My feelings on the country are partial. My feeling on military service is not.

This is part of why I suggest that every warrior develop a meditation practice and regularly engage in serious contemplation and introspection. You have to know your own mind. You have to know what you believe and why you believe it and, as I noted, to what extent you REALLY believe it.

As a Buddhist, it can be certain that Musashi had such a practice. The writings of Takuan Soho, which may have been letters to Musashi and/or his contemporary Yagyu Munenori, go into a depth of detail that practice with the sword must be, in some sense, a meditative practice.

Plato argued that the Philosopher must be a warrior. He also suggested that the warrior must be, in some sense, a philosopher. If you're going to hold a value so dear you would kill for it and possibly die for it, it is crucial that we understand where our values come from. As easy as it to say, "We must fight for Justice", Plato wrote hundreds of pages which seem to make it clear that very few of us have any real idea what Justice really is.

Yagyu Munenori wrote of the "life giving sword[21]" and suggested that the purpose of the weapon isn't to kill men, but to end Evil. Unfortunately, there is no evil under the sky save that in the hearts of men and the hands guided by that heart. So, if we are going to kill men and defend "Good" we'd better be certain we will have no regrets afterward when we learn our "partial feeling" was completely in error.

The second habit required when one holds incomplete beliefs is the adoption of contingency plans. Every plan the military makes considers the possibility that our understanding is incomplete. As a result, those plans contain clauses that "If we find this, we will do that." When we hold partial feelings, we must have plans and provisions that come in to play when we discover which of the possibilities we half believe in is "things as they are."

---

[21] THE LIFE GIVING SWORD by Yagyu Munenori, tr. William Scott Wilson, Kodansha, 2003

Again we are brought to the first precept. We discussed there our acceptance that we will always have blind spots and errors in our understanding. But we are resolved to accept things as they are no matter how inconvenient that is to our self image or our view of the world.

Likewise, when our feelings are partial or incomplete, we must consider how we will act when reality comes down on one side or the other and makes one belief complete. We must have contingency plans. "Trust, but verify." Be prepared when one verifies our trust was given in error, act on the way things are, not on that fiction our trust hoped for.

General James Mattis gave us a good rule to follow: "Be polite, be professional, but have a plan to kill everybody you meet."

We are obliged by the human condition to act on impartial feelings. I suspect most men are good and mean well for their fellows. But I always carry myself as if among secretive enemies. I cannot rely on my suspicion that men are good and let my guard down, exposing those I love to the wrath or opportunity of those few corrupt souls.

It is also essential that I understand that I might be the one mistaken in those matters I have not had the opportunity to thoroughly explore. I have a teacher with a virulent hatred of al-Islam. He has never spoken with Muslims, never lived among them, and I have no idea which "alternative press" he gets his ideas from in this regard as he is not "racist" or so bigoted in any other arena of which I am aware. But this hatred has led him to support the idea of burning the Holy Book of soldiers I have deployed with to fight against Islamic Terrorism.

His feeling is no way partial; his feeling is simply wrong.

This sort of error can only be avoided by vigorous study and contemplation. Being a warrior is neither for the lazy of body nor of mind.

Though it is inevitable that we will only partially understand some situations, we must never act with doubt as to our course of action. While we can intellectually accept that circumstances might evolve in such a way that find the course of action we have selected is inappropriate, until that evidence arises and our conviction changes, we must commit to our actions totally.

If we cannot analyze a situation deeply enough to commit completely to an action, it is better to wait and let that situation evolve and allow our understanding to increase. Proceeding with hesitation almost always leads to disaster.

We must especially never rely on a partial feeling as to our own intentions and actions.

Even as we must be prepared to act in earnest when we learn a friend was actually working against us, we must accept the equally real possibility that those we see as adversaries might turn out to be good, honest men with whom we could be friends or, at least, no longer foes.

As warriors, we must acknowledge the need to be prepared for the unpleasant experience of learning that our worst suspicions might be the reality we live in. Especially examine and test your own capabilities and refuse to depend on anything but the most solid proof that you are physically, mentally prepared to walk the Way Alone.

Precept Four: Think Lightly Of Yourself But Seriously Of The World

In a thousand years, no one will remember your name.

In a thousand years, the cultures our children live in and consider themselves to be products of will bear no resemblance to the world we live in now.

That is the measure of exactly how important you are.

The Roman Emperor Marcus Aurelius wrote, "Short then is the time every man lives, and small the nook of the earth where he lives; and short, too, the longest posthumous fame.[22]" Your impact might live forever. We do not know the name of that first man who smelted iron, but we built civilizations on that knowledge. The world lasts forever, and what you do might "echo in eternity." But who you are will be lost one day.

As warriors, our investment in training and fitness almost inevitably leads to ego and even hubris. Hubris was the name the Greeks gave to that pride that bordered on madness. We've all known it. It's impossible to embrace the study of violence and not, at some point, realize you are one of the most bad ass mother fuckers on the planet. Even if you're not.

Ego can, however, have its drawbacks.

---

[22] MEDITATIONS by Marcus Aurelius tr. George Long, Barnes and Nobel, 2003 (Specifically III. 10)

I was nearly fifty when I picked up the sword again. During the thirty years I had not trained with that weapon, I had served in Iraq and Afghanistan and won my spurs with the most skilled cavalry squadron in the US Army. I had been a Border Patrol Agent and an Air Marshal, proving my skill with a handgun was far beyond the norm. I was, without a doubt, the most experienced warrior on that field where grown men of the 21st Century played at being knights and vikings.

I was slow with a sword, clumsy with my shield. It was very difficult for me to set my ego aside and learn from kids less than half my age who had never been in a real fight. I did not take myself or my supposed prowess lightly at all and so my training suffered.

The admonition in this precept isn't just about training. If we place ourselves at the center of our world, it becomes difficult to justify the sacrifices warriors can be called upon to make. If we place ourselves at the center of the world, it becomes difficult to not take the accidents of events personally. Taking such things personally can give rise to a perceived need to defend the ego when it is not under attack. Worse, it can add the burden of defending the ego to the already enormous burden of protecting one's loved ones.

In the end, the warrior always fights for something outside of himself. He takes his own life less seriously than he does the causes for which he fights. I've met young men who think their own existence is crucial to all they know and see the possibility of their own extinction as somehow tragic. These young men inevitably fail to stand for anything. In their conviction that their lives are to be taken seriously, they fail to have any real significance. Their ego leaves them in the condition of infants.

We will see this idea again in later precepts: ego can be a vulnerability that requires energy to defend it, distracting us from more legitimate adversaries. Being committed first to the Way and then to those we defend, or first to those we defend and then the Way, leaves little time and energy to devote to the needs of the ego.

In short, over-involving our own ego and sense of importance always makes a task more difficult and interferes with our understanding of any given situation. When I returned to the sword, the difficulty in training seriously was created by my inability to take myself lightly. If we enter actual conflict with our thoughts on our need to protect our ego, we may find we are too distracted to respond appropriately to the situation.

This is why Musashi says to think lightly of yourself.

But we are also counseled to take the world seriously. Our footprint in history is almost certain to be a small one. Even so, our deeds impact those around us and ripple outwards whether for good or ill. While mostly ignoring the effect the world has on our ego, we must remain cognizant of the effects our deeds have on the greater world around us.

That my parents never approved of the martial course my life has taken must be examined, accepted, then pushed aside so it does not slow my hand in battle. My life can be taken lightly. But that the world draws closer to what Guillaume Faye calls "The Convergence Of Catastrophes" guides me, it pushes me to train and to study and to teach.

My own fate is certain; I will one day die. It is the uncertain fates of my sons and the sons of my sons and, yes, their sons that I consider more closely. Of course, they, too, will die, but what will the world make of their lives? What becomes of my tribe as the empire dies and the oil runs out and the weather grows more and more extreme?

The world is more important than you are and the reasons to train and struggle and fight are contained within it rather then being contained entirely within yourself. This is why the warrior, in the end, always risks personal extinction to preserve his people or his ideals. The warrior considers himself, to a great degree, expendable. The world is not.

I'm a crazy, tree-hugging, dirt worshipping type. I'm all about recycling and clean water and Mother Earth. But I don't think that is entirely what Musashi is talking about. When Musashi refers to "the world," he really means everything that is outside of ourselves.

When I was a police officer, I often heard officers say, "The most important part of the job is to be alive to go home at night." I disagreed. I still disagree. The most important part of the job was to make sure my partner went home at night. The second most important part of the job was to make sure none of the people I had sworn to protect were failed. Even know I wonder if I had that backwards.

Luckily, I had a great partner, Willie Blackmon, and my back was always covered and I was always better protected than he was. He is a great warrior, not a simple cop, and together we did a lot of crazy shit that men seeking only to go home at night might not have done. We took our oath seriously. We took each other seriously. We took the world seriously. We thought lightly of ourselves.

Being invested first in your own survival rarely leads to a following of the Way. The warrior takes too many risks, spends too much time in the company of those who would kill him to be invested in himself seriously. If you wish to live forever, grow fat and old, be surrounded by luxury and comfort, you should become a merchant. The warrior too often lives in the dirt, alone and wounded, suffering and fighting for causes outside of himself.

The warrior cannot take himself seriously. He cannot see himself as vital to anything because he knows that he will pass from this life at any moment. It is the world he takes seriously; everything that is not him and especially, perhaps, those things that might have some permanence, his family line, his tribe, his nation, his culture, his reputation, his code, the earth itself.

Most of us are not saints and buddhas. Our "worlds" might be limited by our compassion for the stranger or our affection for our own tribe. The natural environment, however, is something we all share and depend on. There is only one global water supply and poisoning water in China poisons that supply for all of us. There is only one atmosphere and poisoning the air in California poisons it for all of us.

Thinking seriously of the world has to encompass both the people we claim as ours and the natural environment.

The warrior must consider where his ego is most vulnerable and how he can make it impervious so that he need no longer take himself so seriously. Give some thought to exactly how much of the world matters to you. We live in a dying empire. Like that first man to make iron and then had to decide whether to fashion a plow or a sword, we must know what impact we hope our lives pass on to the world that follows the convergence of catastrophes.

Precept Five: Avoid Attachment To Desire For As Long As You Live

Musashi's religion was that mixture of Shinto and Buddhism that pervades Japan even today. He corresponded with some of the great names in Zen Buddhism in the period during which he lived and, in books and movies, is often said to be the student of the great Takuan Soho.

The first of the Buddha's four noble truths is that life is hard. The second is that suffering is caused by attachment. Most westerners see "desire" as connoting a sexual thing. For the Buddhists and Musashi, desire is simply any passionate wanting.

When Musashi wrote this precept, he was living in a cave. As I write this commentary, I am living a spartan existence under the sky, having given up my apartment in order to put that money toward one of my desires. Even so, I have access to luxuries Musashi couldn't imagine from this tablet to pre-cooked food to laundry machines.

I am also far more attached to this desire I am sacrificing for than Musashi would approve of, I think.

What does it mean that we are counseled to be unattached to desire rather than simply to not desire? Even the Buddha didn't tell his followers to never desire, only to avoid being attached. Both recognize that desire is inevitable; human beings want things. Even the desire to attain buddhahood and live the life of a bodhisattva is a desire and a monk must find a way to remain detached from that desire in order to achieve that desire.

You and I now stand in the same place, we desire to be successful warriors who develop our prowess and protect what we love. We are now counseled to engage in a headlong passionate pursuit of that aim, but without being attached to any notion or success or failure.

Since desire is normal and inevitable, we must instead learn to possess all desire without attachment. That is, we must acknowledge we want something, but never allow that something to possess us even if we come to possess it. We will launch into endeavors, chase what we desire and, very often, we will fail. When we fail, we will be crippled if we find that attachment to the outcome has wounded our ego. We must instead be prepared to work and sacrifice and then walk away from the outcome if that outcome is pulling us down.

That is what "detachment from desire" means.

Since being attached to outcome involves our egos, it is inevitably accompanied by fear. The fear of humiliation and a bruised ego is greater than the fear of death for many people. Polls show that fear of public speaking outranks the fear of death in a majority of Americans; the risk of humiliation is greater than the risk of actual extinction.

This fear is a distraction from the Way. When our thoughts are embedded in the outcome and not fully present on the course we have chosen, our progress suffers and we bring that failure closer to reality.

We must be prepared not only to walk away from failure unscarred and ready to begin again, but we must recognize that we cannot become attached even to our successes. Success is, after all, always only temporary. If you build a dream, you must fuel it, repair it where it is dented, protect it from adversaries and always be ready to walk away when preserving the dream is no longer worth the struggle required.

When I teach people to shoot, I often have to explain that the outcome is, in many ways, out of our hands. The laws of physics and the nature of ballistics is not subject to our desire. What we do control is how we stand, how we grip the weapon, how we align the sights, how we develop our sight picture, how we squeeze the trigger. We are unattached to the outcome. We do not control whether we hit the target once the round is fired. So we focus on what we do control and concentrate on what we are doing. Inevitably, when we control ourselves and handle our weapons properly, the outcome is much what we seek. But even so we must not become attached or the frustration of missing or being flushed with the pride of hitting will hinder our further efforts.

We are here now. The outcome is in a future that remains out of our hands.

This sounds easy for a businessman facing bankruptcy when you consider that the warrior's outcome is either life or death. It can be difficult not to be attached to an outcome that involves your extinction and danger to your family and tribe.

An old veteran once tried to explain to me that every soldier chooses one of two roads: the road to life or the road to death. A soldier insisting that he is on the road to life, that he will survive and return home and that survival is his highest goal (that police officer asserting that his number one priority is going home at the end of his shift), will hesitate when he should act. His desire to survive puts him in greater danger as he seeks his own survival when he should be seeking victory. The road to death, however, is that course chosen by the soldier who recognizes the danger and accepts that he is already dead. Being dead, he is free to act, free to fight bravely, free to sacrifice for his comrades. With his thoughts untroubled by fear and the desire to live, he is paradoxically more likely to survive and to win.

Being attached to the outcome of a life and death struggle will slow you down and get you killed.

Another famous book of samurai wisdom, the HAGAKURE, says this, "The way of the samurai is found in death. When it comes to either/or, there is only the quick choice of death. It is not particularly difficult. Be determined and advance. To say that dying without reaching one's aim is to die a dog's death is the frivolous way of sophisticates. When pressed with the choice of life or death, it is not necessary to gain one's aim. We all want to live and, in large part, we make our logic according to what we like."[23]

The author of the HAGAKURE, Yamamoto Tsunetomo, lived about ten years after Musashi. Whereas Musashi lived during a time of war as the Tokugawa Shogunate consolidated its power, Tsunetomo lived during a time of peace (except for a rebellion by the Ainu people) and, as far as we know, never fought a battle or a duel. After serving as a clerk for years, he retired to a monastic life and took the name Jocho.

It is difficult when I read this passage from HAGAKURE to not see it as a suicidal mindset. I am not a fan of Tsunetomo but I see a lesson echoing Musashi alongside this point about death. "When pressed with the choice of life or death, it is not necessary to gain one's aim." I think most modern readers would see that as permission to break and run when further pursuit of one's aim becomes dangerous.

The worse interpretation, the one I fear is more accurate, is that Tsunetomo thinks we should be more excited to die in battle than we are about what we die for. He is very much attached to his desire for such a death even after he has renounced the sword and become a monk.

The ronin is not sworn to a Lord or any principle that he does not choose for himself. He is certainly not out to impress history with a great story of his meaningless death. When the time comes to cast his life

[23] HAGAKURE: THE BOOK OF THE SAMURAI by Yamamoto Tsunetomo tr. William Scott Wilson, Kodansha International 1991 (I took some liberties with punctuation and emphasis in bold.)

aside "as though it meant nothing" he will do so, but he will not do so before that moment out of a conviction that the only good samurai is a dead samurai.

Every warrior should accept from the outset that death is inevitable and, in my opinion, a death pursued in the field (even though we make our adversary work for it) is better than the death that awaits us in hospitals surrounded by tired relatives forced to make terrible decisions on our behalf. But as I enter my mid-fifties, it seems more and more that my desire not to die in bed means nothing to the universe. I have a desire to live and to fight. I will learn to be untroubled and unattached to the outcome of that fight. Even victory and long life can be a burden should we be attached to a desire for a good death.

Suicide was acceptable to the samurai and the Stoics under many circumstances. But never as a way of escaping the pains and discomforts of life. The warrior's death must serve his chosen cause or come as a natural consequence of life being what it is.

For the warrior who acknowledges very few trivial activities and pursues the sword, GO, and playing LEGO on the floor with a child with equal passion and urgency, there are few causes that allow simply quitting as a real alternative. Being attached to the outcome, whether success or failure, is nothing when set against the mountain of duty and the struggle to be proficient warriors, reliable brothers, and good fathers.

The way of the samurai is found in the acceptance of reality, the recognition that one day our failure will lead to our extinction, and our resolve that serving the good and following the Way never yield to the desire for a particular outcome.

In a way, being attached to an outcome is a slippery slope that leads us to violate the first precept. When we work for a goal and then fail, we might cling to the emotion that failure brings and refuse to accept the reality of the situation that has evolved. Clinging to our desire for a certain outcome and a certain reality, we fail to learn the lessons our failure might have brought to us.

This is why men make excuses when they fail; they cannot embrace the reality that their own weakness or error brought about failure, they must insist there was some other cause. They insist reality is not as it truly is and reject the opportunity to improve themselves and correct their own defects. It can be difficult to be attached to reality more than one is attached to outcomes and ego.

Then again, the slogan "The way of Bushido is death" was used by the Empire of Japan to encourage young men to throw their lives away almost frivolously during the Great Pacific War of our grandfathers. Not every defeat is extinction for the modern ronin. There are struggles where our defeat reshapes the world without ending it. More, we sometimes retreat in the face of an enemy which thinks we are broken in order to tend our wounds, sharpen our swords and engage anew. We might be fanatics; we are not wasteful of our own lives any more than we are wasteful of our resources.

Tsunetomo's attitude is further explained in passages where he counsels that vengeance is best achieved by "forcing one's way into a place and being cut down." Such an attitude is foolish and reckless and, no matter how brave it must seem to be willing to die for nothing, the good is served best by knowing when and how to act in the moment. His obsession for rushing in and being killed is not sound tactically or strategically.

As it is not sound tactically or strategically, I'd argue that it is not, for the warrior, sound morally.

Our lives can be seen as a campaign where we learn from our defeats and failures so as to secure our goals through other means at other times. But we do not batter our heads and hearts against obstacles that cannot be moved out of our attachment to an outcome, attachment to a reality that we desire but does not exist.

We often see this in men's relationships with women. Having lost her interest and her passion, he tries harder to be what she says she wants only to see her desire wane further. He doesn't understand that desire cannot be negotiated and that only by understanding and accepting the new reality that he had a hand in creating can he move on and find himself again. Instead, he labors under the delusion that he can deny this reality and recreate the outcome, or re-establish conditions that once existed but have now passed, to which he is attached.

I speak as one who has failed at relationships far, far more often than I have succeeded. In each case, I recognized my failures, sought to correct them, but, in the end, had no choice but to accept that I had failed and both she and I had to move on. I could love her after our lives together ended, but I could not remain attached to that life and that reality once it had passed.

Even our greatest successes will be incomplete and contain lessons that we can only absorb fully to the extent we accept the new situation exactly as it is without reference to our desires for and our attachment to an expected outcome.

On a long enough timeline, you are dead because of failure. Accept that and plan your life, the pursuit of your desires accordingly. If it isn't worth your life, cast it away and even if it is, avoid being attached to your success or failure, ready always to rise and struggle.

Another passage from HAGAKURE: "When we calmly think of death morning and evening and are in despair, we are able to gain freedom in the way of the samurai. Only then can we fulfill our duty without making mistakes in life." To follow the way alone, we must push aside our attachment to an outcome in order to focus our full efforts on the fight before us. Being unattached to an outcome, we can accept reality as it is and address it on the proper terms without fear.

The Way is not about an outcome. It is the "Way of Walking Alone", not the "Way Of Finally Reaching Someplace Where You Are Alone." You have attained nothing until such time as you die and have lived a life in accordance with your code. The Way is a path with no destination other than extinction. To be attached to an outcome at any time before your death is to lose sight of the Way and to be focused on that outcome.

Precept Six: Do Not Regret Anything That You Have Done

Again, let us first discard what this precept does not say. Musashi does not exhort us to impeccable moral behavior but insists that being human, we will err, we will make mistakes, we will choose the wrong action. And Musashi insists also that, when we do, we do not spend a moment in regret for the mistake made or the pain caused.

Such regret accomplishes nothing. It does not further the warrior on the Way and it does not correct whatever injustice the action created.

When I was a child of six or seven, I made a terrible mistake.

Some older children told me that a boy, I do not remember his name, had been picking on my sister. Their suggestion was that I should beat him up to somehow set the world right.

I confronted him and in my memory he has blonde hair and is wearing a blue shirt and he smiles as he denies that he did anything to my sister. My sister, too, denies anything happened. The crowd continues exhorting me to action.

I punched him in the face.

That punch broke his glasses.

I wonder sometimes what else it broke. Was there some terrible echo of that childish misdeed?

I can never atone for that deed. But I also cannot carry it around as a regret.

It is possible that Musashi genuinely meant we should cut and walk away[24]. Any wrong doing, any error is unfortunate but leads only to worse and worse outcomes if we then wallow in regret. Regret is a waste of our time and pulls us from the path. We should leave others to their suffering, even if we are responsible, and proceed with our own journey.

It is possible that is exactly what Musashi meant.

That outlook does most of us no good and I am not at all certain I can embrace it. I am on this path for my own reasons just as you are, but I hold to this old-fashion idea that my conduct will be of benefit to people and not harm.

The warrior, being devoted to accepting the world as it really is, seeks to act always in harmony with what is good and right. In those situations where what is good and right cannot be attained, it is sometimes necessary to simply do what is best.

It can be difficult for the warrior to accept that he is not in complete control of many situations. We train and prepare for the various aspects of struggle but no matter how much effort we exert, there are factors outside of our control. This must serve to preserve us from hubris as well as from regret.

Making excuses and pushing aside our responsibility for a decision or an action that has an

---

[24] Kiri-sute Gomen was a samurai's right to kill a peasant for minor offenses or none at all. Apparently, new swords were sometimes tested or demonstrated in this manner. The expression used is often translated as "to cut and walk away."

imperfect outcome isn't acceptable. But accepting reality as it is requires us to set aside our ego and accept that every outcome, whether positive or negative, contains elements completely outside of our control.

When events do have a negative outcome, it is crucial that we analyze the situation and determine to what extent exactly that outcome was truly influenced by our decisions. The warrior seeks to train and prepare and studies to understand the world in order to have greater control over outcomes.

In the military, we conduct After Action Reviews after a training event or a mission's completion. According to Army Publication TC 25-20, the purpose of the AAR is to discover "what happened, why it happened, and how to sustain strengths and improve on weaknesses." The individual warrior should be similarly involved in periods of reflection where he analyzes what he has done, why and how he might have secured a more perfect outcome.

During this brutal, honest assessment, the warrior finds solutions to his shortcomings whether those be a poorly chosen word or deed or an incomplete understanding of the situation. Either way, there is no room for regret, only for continual improvement.

While everyone is familiar with Marcus Aurelius's MEDITATIONS, his fellow Stoic Philosophers, Epictetus and Seneca, also kept journals and counseled their students to do the same. Seneca in particular recommended a nightly practice of reviewing the day for missed opportunities to do good and those times when we failed and our own efforts to good were imperfect or absent.

This is a tool that could help us follow Musashi's precept if approached with a sincere intent to make right the wrongs we will inevitably commit. Because when the warrior discovers his words or actions have not benefited his cause, he is not served by any feeling of regret, but only by acting to set the situation right.

In the modern age, we too often find corporations and politicians expressing their regret for the outcome of some misdeed, sometimes all the while denying any responsibility for the misdeed in order to pre-empt litigation. It is too easy to say "I'm sorry" and imagine that such an expression of regret some how returns the world to balance or at least absolves the apologist and excuses him from any further action.

Since error is unavoidable, it becomes necessary for me to find another path to avoid regret. The warrior has to recognize that being consumed by the Past, whether pride or regret, is detrimental to the Now. In this respect, Musashi again gives us good counsel, regret is not a burden a warrior can bear for long.

Refusing to simply be heartless and never regret any mistake, I am left casting about in Musashi's culture and life for other possibilities and I find one so drastic, so final that it is also nearly unthinkable as anything other than a clue to help us find our way.

Some samurai, when their errors were so great they felt they could never recover their reputation or their honor, would commit seppuku; ritual suicide. Rather than issue an apology that might ring empty, their sincerity was expressed through the act of inflicting a terrible cruel death upon themselves.

While I can't be an advocate of this either, I do see a path that can lead us away from regret without being callous to those we injure mistakenly: atonement.

When we realize we have taken an action that is not in line with our goals, we are not obligated to think of that deed as "done" while the suffering it causes remains. Simply expressing regret is meaningless. Action must be taken to set things right when it was our action that set things wrong in the first place.

Such action must be sincere and appropriate. While we are obligated to fix what we break, we are not obligated to gild tarnished brass after we have cleaned it. Just as there are those who imagine they can absolve themselves of their misdeeds through simple apologies, there are those with a victim mindset that will never be satisfied when they find themselves wronged or even just imagine they have been insulted.

It is not always possible to satisfy those we have genuinely wronged and we are even less likely to satisfy those who always imagine themselves the victim. Regret could make you their slave as they find newer and bigger (and too often meaningless or imagined) offenses for you to atone for.

Sometimes this is the nature of the person offended. Sometimes it is the nature of the offense. Simply returning stolen goods is not a full atonement for robbery. Could even suicide or execution be a full atonement for the murder of an innocent?

Still, sincere atonement is the only course I can personally adopt in relation to this precept. Regret is an emotion without any upside. Musashi is absolutely right when he advises us to never let regret rest in our psyches for even an instant. It follows that we can be perfect, we can be callous, or we can refuse to let our mistakes remain a hindrance to ourselves or others.

Also, the warrior does not regret the outcome of his deeds because he is not attached to those outcomes. He does what he can, always seeking to follow the Way and do what is best for the causes he serves and must not regret an outcome to which he is not attached.

Many times, regret occurs when we miss an opportunity or take some action that we realize is not in our own best interest. If we miss a day we were supposed to train for good reason, there is still no use for regret. If we do not have good reason, we can only find a way to minimize the harm we have done to ourselves.

Carrying regret around only compounds our error.

Regret can only exist when we do wrong and prefer to carry that burden when we could refuse it. As warriors, we carry many burdens and all of them are of our choosing.

It becomes necessary for the warrior to examine his life constantly. We examine and adjust our training routines, we must also examine and adjust our ethics and values and relationships. That our values bring us into conflict with others is to be expected from time to time. There should be no regret attached to this.

When we discover, however, that our thinking, or our relationships bring us to a point in our lives where we must meditate on our regrets and address our deeds too often in light of error and regret, it could be an indicator that we need to excise such people and such attitudes from our lives.

If our commitment to the good and the right consistently brings us into conflict with those we love, we must choose, without regret, which we will keep and which we will sacrifice for the Way.

We choose our own burdens. We must choose as wisely as we can.

Precept Seven: Never Be Envious

I do not speak Japanese and have to rely on translators. I sometimes wonder if the Japanese language has separate words for "jealousy" and "envy" and, if so, which word Musashi used here and what our translator thought he meant.

"Jealousy" is a desire to keep what is ours. It means being vigilant and protective of what we see as ours. "Envy" is the desire for what another possesses, or, worse, a feeling of resentment attached to that desire.

When I say I am jealous of my girl, I mean I am unwilling to share her. When I say I am envious of her, I mean that I wish I was as smart as she is.

For this reason, even though this precept is most often presented as "Never be Jealous" I am addressing it as: Never be Envious.

Envy is a result, the negative result, of comparing ourselves and our situations to what others are experiencing. The positive result is inspiration. The obligation we then incur, if we seek to follow the Way Alone as advocated by Musashi, is to transform the negative feeling of envy into either apathy or inspiration.

The warrior does not look at another's success and want to take it from them and make it their own. The warrior sees in another what is possible and then seeks to build it for himself in his own life. This is inspiration and not mere envy.

But as I write, I am always thinking of my tribe, and my adversaries aren't always personal but are often forces and people who simply oppose my tribe and, when not eager to destroy us, are at least willing to see us destroyed.

When the tribe's adversaries possess resources that your tribe needs, it isn't possible to meditate, reflect, and then dispense with your need and watch your tribe perish. Looking at the oil possessed by the countries of the Middle East might make us wish we had that oil. But that oil will run out and envy of their position accomplishes nothing. We should instead allow that to inspire us to trade with them and develop alternatives and our own resources. It is not an excuse for war.

But what about water? As the population grows and industrialization poisons the global water supply, my tribe's need for water might lead us into conflict with another tribe that does have sufficient water. Again, we can trade, we can negotiate. But if that fails, it is impossible to cast aside that desire and do without water. It then becomes necessary to dispense with mere envy and engage in conquest. But conquest is never accomplished without the sacrifice of much of what we hold dear. It is a trade with fate, at best.

That said, it isn't likely that a basic need such a food, water, or shelter becomes the object of our envy or our jealousy. We are much more likely to find ourselves envious, not of what another has, but of the nature of what they have compared to our own situation. I have a truck, he has a bigger, newer truck. I have water, he has wine. I have beans and rice, he has steak and eggs.

These envies can always be transformed into inspiration. It is far more difficult to handle the envy that is rooted in: "I have respect from my tribe; he has far more respect and the attention of every beautiful woman within a thousand miles."

In a situation like this, it becomes necessary to evaluate the opinions and values of those around us. If you are not respected and appreciated by your tribe and family, you must first ask the hard questions about whether you warrant respect and affection. If you can honestly assert that your conduct and your deeds warrant respect and affection but you feel unappreciated, it might be that you are in the company of those who do not hold values that match your own.

In my squadron, I was respected for my intelligence and my sense of humor and my skill as a medic. Among strangers, my sense of humor was often seen as jarring and my intelligence as snobbery and my skills as a medic were seen as arrogance. When among those who could be won over by prowess in their fields, I was usually quickly accepted, but it happened more than once that someone found nothing in me that they could tolerate.

Perhaps it IS arrogance but this feeling is usually mutual. Only a fool rejects the strengths and virtues I bring to the fight. I do not desire the respect or affection of fools. If I did require their respect, I might find myself giving in to peer pressure and sacrifice my other values to that need for their respect.

Being envious of another's social standing is, then, a sacrifice of our own values and our sense of self to the judgement of others. If we can stand with perfect certitude that we are deserving of the respect and affection of those around us but we do not have it, then the indictment is not against us but against them.

That the values of the warrior are not appreciated in the empire is one reason why we find ourselves walking the Way alone.

Envy is a hindrance. It distracts us from our own accomplishments and impedes our relationships with others. Our obligation is then to consider these three possible alternatives: apathy, inspiration, conquest.

Analyze your relationships with those who possess what you do not and begin planning for how you can match their situation and better yourself. Especially analyze how much of your jealousy is rooted in still being attached to outcomes you cannot control.

Precept Eight: Never Let Yourself Be Saddened By A Separation

Despite the appearance of romance in Yoshikawa's novel and the trilogy of movies based on it, there is no evidence that Musashi had any close friends or a love interest. When Musashi writes about walking alone, he truly means alone[25]. I doubt he loved anyone to the extent that he was ever saddened by a separation from anyone. From my perspective, this is a very sad comment on the man's life. I much prefer the stories of Yoshikawa.

I have two sons. The oldest was only eight when I went to Iraq and then he was eleven and his brother only a few months old when I went to Afghanistan. We spoke on the phone often and I was able to send him gifts ordered online. Such is the reality of war in the 21st Century.

We both struggled with the sadness of our separation, but my sadness was tinged with the knowledge that I was missing days I would never get back. There are still times I find myself aching for those days.

I've said in previous comments that the values and worldview of the warrior are not appreciated in the

---

[25] It is unclear to what extent Musashi's students travelled with him. It has long been a habit for a warrior or a nobleman to travel with a retinue of supporters but, if he were unaccompanied by peers, he might still refer to himself as being alone. But it was also common for a samurai on his warrior pilgrimage to travel solo.

Empire of Nothing. I've known many soldiers who found upon their return to the world that the world had moved on and left them behind. Their marriages ended, their relationships with everyone they had left behind were, in some cases, simply wrecked beyond repair.

War changes men and some times those changes remake us as people so that those who once loved us can love us no longer. Much of this is the soldier's fault in many cases. It isn't easy to come back to a woman who no longer understands us because they do not understand what we have done and beg for the time to open up or the understanding that we never will.

As we walk the Way, we will find again and again that there are very few who understand our path and even fewer willing to walk it with us. Many will try. Many will make sincere efforts to support us as we pursue this Way. But the Way is hard not only for the warrior but for all of those who hurt when he cannot and those for whom his sacrifice becomes their sacrifice.

There will be many instances when the warrior must choose between the Way and those who cannot walk it with him. If the fear of separation and the sadness that comes with it weighs on the warrior, he will not follow the Way.

I do not mean to suggest that the warrior must be made of stone and incapable of feeling. But he must not allow his attachments to pull him away from his cause and his feelings and fear of sadness to unmake him.

In recent years, there has been a resurgence of interest in the philosophy of stoicism. One of the tenets of that philosophy is that a wise man must master his emotions and realize that while events may occur, our feelings about those events are of our own making. In this fashion, many of Musashi's precepts are calls to stoicism.

None more than this one.

We have examined precepts against being attached to our desires and against jealousy, but now Musashi reminds us that even our most human relationships are a distraction if we indulge in sadness because of them. When I was in Iraq, I often looked forward to talks with my son. But I never allowed a feeling of sorrow or expectation to intrude into my thoughts during a mission.

It can be pleasant to think of those we love who are not with us. But if we are to accept things exactly as they are, we must proceed even in their absence with all of our will, exactly as we commit to every other aspect of being a warrior.

In these essays I hope I have never made this path sound easy. It isn't possible for a healthy human being with normal human attachments to just decide he is no longer going to be saddened by separation. Even Musashi would recognize that for individuals less exceptional than he is, these precepts take work. They are a struggle.

It might be that Musashi would then dismiss those of us who cannot immediately embrace the fanaticism of his Do. But if we find any value in his teaching, we will proceed and find ways to understand his precepts in our lives.

Separation takes many forms. We leave our families when we start to make our own. Our children then, in turn, often leave us. Warriors find themselves summoned to battlefields far from home. And, finally, death takes comrades and loved ones.

It is so much easier to write and meditate upon our own deaths than it is of those we truly love. I am prepared for my death. But when counseled to "not be saddened by a separation" I immediately think of that great separation that occurs at the death of another.

The warrior must be prepared in the face of every such separation to carry on with his mission, to push further down this path. Sadness can easily grow into a mind-numbing grief and lead to self-extinction. Sadness must be examined, dealt with, and discarded. Even the great Buddhist patriarchs were unable to simply accept separation and move on without reflection.

A story told about a Chinese Buddhist sage named Chuang Tzu tells how his wife passed away and he was visited by a friend who found him playing a drum and singing. The friend saw this as disrespect for his beloved wife and told him so. That prompted Chuang Tzu to explain that he had already mourned his wife. That he had wept and wept but then he had reflected that she was not his and that the universe had once existed without her and that all things pass away. To continue weeping would be, in his words, "to proclaim myself ignorant of this fact."

This then, might be a model for our own exercise of this precept. The natural, inevitable sadness of separation must be expressed and examined. Then we must let it go in order to continue our mission. We must find a way to rest comfortably in the will of the universe, unattached to outcomes and accepting those things we cannot control.

Much of that way, I think, is found in the advice Musashi gives in the sixth precept where we are counseled not to regret what we have done. I think this precept reminds us that we sometimes have occasion to regret what we have not done.

Preparing for the inevitable separations: death, divorce, simply growing apart, it isn't enough to simply harden our hearts and embrace that being alone. We have an opportunity now to do and say what we will regret having omitted after a separation.

My grandfather was hospitalized for many weeks before his death. Before he drove us to the hospital, he walked around the house making a list of the things he had to repair when he got home. I sat with him much of the time, reading and watching MAGNUM PI during afternoon reruns.

I had just gotten out of the army (for the first time) and had enrolled at the university. When it was time for classes to start, I left intending to be back as often as I could, but leaving my grandparents, who were normally fit and strong and self-reliant, alone for the time being.

The last words I ever said to my grandfather were, "I'll be back."

His last words to me were, "I'll be here."

Not the worst of partings; I know we said we loved each other and made plans for what we'd do when he was out and we had time to work on the house. But what might I have done differently had I known that "I'll be here" wasn't exactly true?

My sister died on July 6, 2018 at the age of 50 after a 35 year long battle with one cancer after another. We would joke about her timing when she developed breast cancer while I was deployed to Iraq. I know she somehow arranged it on purpose so that she could be the center of our mother's worry when I was deployed.

Knowing that one day one of us would die before the other, we took note of the fact that every time we said "good-bye" it was possibly the last time. In truth, I do not remember the last time she and I stood together in the same room, but I think it was when we painted rocks at her kitchen table for one of her eternal art projects.

Its almost a cliché to suggest that you tell then ones you love that you love them while you still can.

But tell the ones you love that you love them while you still can. The warrior keeps Death as an advisor at his shoulder whispering "Memento Mori" at every pause. We will not know which chance to say "good-bye" and "I love you" will be the last, so we take every chance.

And being warriors, we are conscious that many times, a separation involves sadness for the other person also. We have their feelings and future in our hands as well. We do not let quarrels come between us and those we love in such a way that this might be their last memory of us.

We prepare for separation before that separation occurs by making sure everyone we care for knows and feels cared for. We do not risk leaving some word unsaid or some deed undone that we might find reason to regret later. We do not leave undone anything that might cause us to be sad at the inevitable separations in a warrior's life

Then we must train and fight unencumbered by sadness.

Precept Nine: Resentment And Complaining Are Not Appropriate For The Warrior Or For Anyone Else

Of all of Musashi's precepts, this one is, I think, among the easiest to understand and put into action. That is the key word: "action."

Consider the other attributes the warrior may have, but, in the end, he is always a man of action.

A warrior accepts things exactly as they are. It rains when he is on the march. He marches. The campaign takes him away from his loved ones. He endures. His government decays into a fetid swamp of corruption and special interests. He obeys.

Or he rebels.

The warrior is a man of action and has no use for those who would substitute words for deeds.

When a man complains, he is hoping that someone else will take pity on his situation and change it. Or he is simply lost, unable to accept the First Precept and somehow lost in a fantasy that reality will bend to his wishes without action on his part if he only expresses his dissatisfaction properly. A warrior will understand that he must act to change that situation himself. He might share his concerns with comrades to discuss their nature and the nature of their solution. When a solution can be divined, the warrior then acts.

A complaint given voice without intent to make a change in circumstances only serves to undermine the morale of those around the complainer. No man has a right to spread his suffering to others. If you have no intent to act and correct a bad situation, complaining only puts that burden to act on others.

More than that, making change requires energy. Complaining is a venting of that energy that results in you having less energy to begin a serious protest and a serious campaign of change.

I've also noticed among some people, especially those who reject the first precept that once they have complained sufficiently, they think they have fulfilled their obligation to actually DO something. They have no intention of acting beyond their loud assertion that things "should be different."

For years now, much of the complaining I have encountered involves the dissatisfaction of those on the left since the 2016 presidential election and the dissatisfaction of those on the right with the dissatisfaction of those on the left. At first, I tried answering questions and addressing other's concerns with my own but I quickly discovered that very few are listening, very few are seeking answers. People seem to have chosen sides and no fact or argument can be tolerated unless it feeds their side.

They eagerly, rabidly reject reality and instead scream their resentment and complaint but DO nothing. Often clinging to that conviction that their whining IS action.

When confronted, they often sarcastically ask if I expect them to blow up the White House or join some Antifa Riot. Yes. If you honestly think democracy is at stake and a tyrant has illegally seized power, why would you not take such action? By complaining are they not inciting others to such action they will not take themselves? If you are unwilling to act, stop suggesting that someone should.

This can never be the way of the warrior. While the masses scream and insult each other, accomplishing nothing, there is little the warrior can do but abide, train, seek his own peace and be prepared when the situation finally evolves into something that requires action. Shouting at an opponent who is not listening, who may be simply incapable of listening, is futile and, since it cannot make change, it does not rise above mere complaint.

A complaint given with the intent to act is a warning.

Resentment comes when a man faces an intolerable situation but will not act. That complaint grows inside his breast into a poison that harms him far more than it does any other. The man is likely to claim that he cannot act. Invariably, he means the forces arrayed against him (his employer, his wife, the courts, the system, society at large) are too great to be overcome. Even so, the certainty of defeat is no excuse for the warrior to refuse to act.

When the situation cannot be changed, the warrior endures or adapts. And he does not waste time lamenting that he has chosen a path for his life that exposes him to discomfort and unpleasantness. Marcus Aurelius stated it this way, "At dawn, when you have trouble getting out of bed, tell yourself, 'I have to do a man's work today. What do I have to complain of if I am going to do the work for which I was born? Or...is THIS what I was created for: to huddle under the blankets and stay warm?"[26]

Marcus Aurelius was also among the first to say, "If you can endure it, stop complaining and endure it. If you can't endure it, stop complaining because the suffering will stop once it kills you."[27]

There is a saying among martial artists that our thoughts and our words follow each other. If your words are filled with complaint, soon your thoughts will be focused on the imperfections of the world and you will lose sight of that beauty that should be our purpose.

Holding tight to that vision of beauty even in the midst of the world's imperfections is how we train ourselves to experience the rainstorm as a gift and not a misfortune.

Another aspect of accepting reality is the recognition that reality is always in flux, always changing. The warrior has to become adept at adapting to these changes as uncomfortable as they may be. Whether it is a simple change in the weather as the day passes or the change in society that seems to have overtaken me as I grow old, I have to adapt to what I cannot change.

---

[26] MEDITATIONS Bk. V v.1
[27] MEDITATIONS Bk. X v.3 (Heavily paraphrased by the author.)

And much complaining can be better addressed with a simple realization that "this, too, shall pass." It won't rain all the time. Will you then complain it is too dry? There is another election around the corner. Will you respect the loser's complaints if you win as you expected them to respect yours?

To drag another Roman Stoic into our exploration, the former slave Epictetus pointed out that while we notice a few bad things, we often miss the myriad of things that are exactly right. In modern psychology, this is known as the "Negativity Bias." People have a tendency to let things of a negative nature have a greater impact on their awareness than positive ones.

A soldier on the move in the rain can obsess over the discomfort in his own boots, or he can consider that it is raining on his enemy, too, and that whoever yields first to the temptation to seek warmth and dryness will be the one unprepared when they find each other.

I do not mean to imply that the fist is always the answer to every wrong. Constructing arguments and explaining why an individual or a group should change their course of action could be all that is required to change an intolerable situation. It is not the sort of complaint that currently goes on so loudly among various political factions, but a counseling and education of sorts intended to make things better for everyone.

Dr. Martin Luther King preached peace and patience as he confronted an evil system determined to hold an entire race down. He did so by example and by his sermons. But he kept a shotgun by the door. In the end, he gave his life for the change he knew was necessary in his homeland. Still, it would be a great misunderstanding to think he ever uttered one word of complaint.

Its also important to note the positive role that discomfort plays in the life and training of the warrior. We lift until our muscles are tired, tap out only when pain forces us to recognize our mistakes, and do so because we are willing to risk the greatest injuries if circumstances require it.

In preparing for these discomforts, the warrior is willing to intentionally make himself uncomfortable. This should serve the purpose of making him immune to complaint. Why complain that there is no food today if you have intentionally gone without food before? Why complain of the cold when you have made a habit of exposing yourself to the extremes of weather?

The Stoics were masters of such preparation. In his LETTERS, Seneca counseled that we set aside a certain number of days and live then as if in abject poverty, eating poor food, wearing rough clothes. Then asking one's self, "Is this the condition I feared?"[28] He even compares this habit to the training of a soldier who
"builds earthworks when there is no enemy around" in preparation for that day when enemies are present.

---

[28] LETTERS FROM A STOIC by Seneca Letter XVIII, v5,6 (Penguin Classics, 1969)

Cato the Younger routinely appeared in the Roman Senate wearing animal skins instead of a toga and was known to eat simply and exercise vigorously. He was known for his integrity and looked down on by many for his refusal to take bribes and thus grease the machinery on which the Republic functioned.

While Cato was not a samurai, the description Plutarch gives of us the senator's death sounds very much like seppuku. Cato thrust his sword into his own abdomen and, when comrades attempted to save him, he reached into the cut with his hands and pulled his entrails out so that his death was certain.[29]

By embracing discomfort when comfort was available: cold baths, sleeping on the ground, fasting, these men prepared themselves for the inevitable discomforts that life can thrust upon any person, but which are inevitable in the life of the warrior. Discomfort must be embraced for the good things it brings so as to inoculate the warrior. This precludes complaining.

The warrior recognizes that his situation is a result of his own choices and that it will be his own choices that sweep away the irritant and bring in a new situation. One such choice the warrior makes in in his words. Like Dr King, the warrior advises, he counsels, he points out to others where he thinks things have gone awry and corrections must be made.

---

[29] THE MAKERS OF ROME: NINE LIVES by Plutarch. (Penguin Classics, 1965)

But he does so in a way that makes it clear his words are a call to action or a warning. Never mere complaint.

In a previous essay, I mentioned the ritual of seppuku. While samurai had many reasons for ending their own lives, one almost common reason was to lodge a complaint. Known as kanshi, a samurai who wished to protest a lord's decision would show his sincerity by making the fatal cut and then appearing before his lord to make his protest. Only after would he expose his wound. There was also a practice known as funshi which was the completion of the ritual to state a samurai's protest against his lord's decision.

Complaining also robs the warrior of an opportunity to become better. There are, after all, situations which seem unendurable and unalterable. We can benefit from the Stoic position here, after all, Stoic has come to mean "uncomplaining" in modern usage.

With that example in mind, we find the warrior has three options when confronted by an intolerable situation. He can change the circumstances, change himself or simply endure. When he finds it necessary to state his dissatisfaction, then discovers acting is impossible and it is necessary to endure, he must release that dissatisfaction and give it neither room nor fuel to grow into resentment. This is what it means to endure.

The very nature of the warrior revolves around these three possibilities. The warrior exists for conflict and for the betterment of the world brought about by clashing with evil and using force to protect or bring about the Good. His training and his prowess is for the purpose of changing himself and the circumstances of those around him.

It is a mistake to take the universe personally. It is a mistake to think our complaints have any real impact on the world.

In the "despair[30]" episode of the TV Series DEADWOOD, Al Swearingen comforts a man complaining by saying, "Pain or damage don't end the world. Or despair. Or fuckin' beatings. The world ends when you're dead. Until then, you got more punishment in store. Stand it like a man. And give some back."

The world will never be completely to your liking. Fight back or make peace with it but never complain.

Stand it like a warrior.

---

[30] DEADWOOD Season 2 Episode 7

Precept Ten: Do Not Let Yourself Be Guided By The Feeling Of Lust Or Love

Musashi was a warrior first and these precepts and this short commentary are written for warriors. In my experience, warriors are the most passionate of men. While there is much of reason in the purpose and choice to train and fight, it is very seldom reason that moves men to actually engage in conflict. In some cases, it is hatred of an "other." It's currently popular to say, "The warrior does not fight because he hates what is in front of him, but because he loves what is behind him."

I say that the warrior fights because he is a warrior. I say that while what we love and what we hate might play some part in the choice of which causes to serve, it is more often accidental, a matter of birth or nationality and circumstance. Many of those who enlisted after the 9/11 attacks were motivated by anger and hatred of an enemy they knew nothing about and a sudden passionate affection for a cause they had never considered the day before.

Those of us who were already carrying a weapon for the state merely saw it as another event in our career as soldiers.

In this precept, Musashi is not telling us to avoid love and lust, though if he ever felt these two emotions, he did an admirable job of never letting them sway him from his course. He is, however, cautioning us that those passions are usually detrimental to good decision making. Any passion is a hindrance in battle, and, in my experience, there is no greater passion than romantic love. Except possibly animal lust.

Musashi has advised us again and again to guard our thoughts and feelings. Since it is impossible to simply not have feelings, and we will not make the attempt to do away with feelings as that violates the first precept, we must then guard our deeds from our feelings.

In the introduction I explained that I write these essays as a "modern day ronin" in the sense that, having carried a weapon for the state, having had a warrior identity formed in that service, I am no longer bound by oath to anyone. Like a ronin, I am "masterless" and, I imagine, so are most of you.

Despite the allure of walking the roads of medieval Japan, dueling for the sake of honing our skill and living by our wits, we find ourselves in the early 21st century instead where such things are made exceedingly difficult. Most of us have families now instead of clans and our native warrior instincts are put in service to them. Our training, our armament, our survival preparations are made toward the end of protecting those we love.

But we have also discussed already the fact that most of us will lose people as we walk the Way, and the ugly truth is that very few people have it in them to walk alongside a warrior. There is a saying that the most difficult job in the army is being a soldier's wife. The divorce rates among soldiers and veterans is so remarkably high for a reason.

For reasons we could argue about for days and never resolve fully, the martial arts and prowess...the Way of The Warrior...is seen as a male prerogative. I even argue it is an obligation for men in ways it is not for women. But in this day when women are trained as infantrymen in the Army and even go on to graduate Ranger School, only a fool can continue to deny that some women are born to be warriors.

That said, I have found that women have a much greater difficulty finding men who can appreciate a woman who is dedicated to the Way of the Warrior if he is not dedicated to the Way as well.

It is the nature of many people to seek validation through the attention paid to them by their partner. Every woman reading this just recoiled from those words asserting that she is, in fact, a strong independent woman who needs no man. A look inside her closet or her underwear drawer or her makeup counter might suggest she is misleading herself.

A woman wants to be chosen over things and measures her self worth and the depth of a man's affection by what he sacrifices for her. Ironically, she also measures the worth of a man by how easily he can refuse her demands with a smile on his face and never lose who he is in his feelings for her. She does not want to be the center of a weak man's world, she wants to hold a place in the heart of a warrior.

The warrior must understand that any partner will say she supports his efforts on the Way but then pout when he spends so much time at the gym and the dojo instead of with her. The warrior will find that his partner resents his dedication to simplicity when she wants luxury.

The warrior loves as anyone does. In these moments when his determination to follow the Way is challenged in the name of Love or Lust, he must follow his true nature. The warrior will be guided by his values and his cause to choose the Way. He must never allow himself to be led by his affection for a woman who does not sincerely understand his path and commit to him as a warrior and not just as the man providing for her future.

We must make our decisions based on our own identity and reasons. I do love my family, but I did not become a warrior out of that love. I became a warrior because of some set of instincts and proclivities in my psyche. Now I must choose how to live.

I do not let love or lust decide if I should train. I train because I am a warrior. I do not let love or lust plan my defenses. I let my understanding of the enemy plan my defenses. I do not let love or lust choose my enemy. My enemy chooses himself when he pits himself against me. I do not let love or lust choose my recreations, even that must be seen in the light of how it adds to my path.

And when engaged in the fight, there is no passion, no love or lust, no anger or hate. There is only you and the adversary and the struggle for an outcome to which we are not attached.

Again and again, the DOKKODO brings us to this point: we are what we are, we do what we do, and nothing else is of such consequence that we allow it to distract us from our nature and the pursuit of the Way. We live in the paradox of defending what we love by not allowing that love to guide our hands.

If the warrior does decide to share his life, he must understand the nature of his partner and put his own nature first. He must resolve from the beginning to be uncompromising on his identity and expect his partner to love him for what he truly is: a warrior.

It might not be enough that she merely accept this part of him, as it is the foundation of all else he is, but her love for him must be firmly rooted in her perception of him AS a warrior. She should not be merely a recreation or a pleasant diversion, she must be an inspiration. Her presence, her nature, her affection must be such that they provide support and refuge and motivation to the warrior.

It is better that she be such a woman that rather than protesting he spends too much time at the gym and on the mat, she notices aloud when the warrior fails to uphold his chosen way. It is best when the warrior simply sees and feels her and recognizes she deserves, not the constant attention of some simpering courtier, but the genuine affection of an authentic man. Seeing this, his drive to improve and walk the way is aided by his desire to fulfill his own nature and his desire to be worthy of her.

Paradoxically, the greatest indicator that she is not such a woman as might be a warrior's lover is that she will expect him to prove he is worthy of her. She must be self-aware enough to reason out that a man can only be what he is and, that while her presence can provide fuel, his desire for her cannot be the foundation of their relationship. She must recognize that a man is a warrior as a result of his own nature and that even her love cannot make a warrior of a bureaucrat; only his own awakening can do that.

Such women are very rare in these early days of the 21st century. The empire does not harbor affection or even much tolerance for that woman who would rather be a warrior's slave than a merchant's mistress.

But if the warrior is to be true to himself and follow this Way, he must not compromise and accept a permanent place for a lesser woman in his life because she will inevitably become a hindrance. The sole measure of a woman's worth in a warrior's life is that who she most truly is serves and inspires his own identity as a warrior.

In this way, his love is not guiding him, but is, instead, a natural consequence of his adherence to the Way.

Lust is a different matter perhaps.

When I write about serious things, I often sound as if there is little enjoyment in life. If you were to ask the men I have deployed with, drank with...chased pussy with...they'd tell you I am one funny motherfucker. I laugh a great deal and have an immense appetite for pleasure.

If you saw the quality of girl I often find myself involved with, you'd think I was incredibly wealthy or had game like you read about in the back of Penthouse magazine.

I do not know if Musashi meant to be as puritanical in his assertion that we not be guided by lust as it might sound. He never married, had no romances that we know of so it is possible his fanaticism was all part of some primeval, pre-internet MGTOW attitude. If so, however, that attitude doesn't suit my own life. I couldn't fake a willingness to be celibate for very long.

With that in mind, I know from experience not to expect the men who might read this to eagerly adopt the attitudes of warrior monks and resolve to never get their dick wet again outside the relationship they form with that loving wife I described earlier.

What this precept does proscribe is that set of attitudes that allow a man's thirst for sex to define him and dictate his actions. Some men are best defined by their skill at romantic conquest just as some men are best defined by their acumen for making money and doing business. A warrior might or might not develop great expertise in these arenas also, but he is defined by his prowess and his capacity to make war.

Neither love nor lust define the warrior.

But do not be surprised to find he excels at both.

Precept Eleven: In All Things, Have No Preferences

Musashi was an extreme individual living on the fringes of an extreme society. At first glance you might see how you also are an extreme individual living on the fringes of an extreme society, but by taking seriously the idea that a man has an obligation to cultivate prowess and strength, you set yourself at the edge of a dying empire instead of near its soft, vulnerable center.

Notice I did not say that you chose this path. I do not think we choose to be warriors. I think it is coded in our psyches by virtue of being the descendants of those men who fed their families by thrusting sharp sticks at the mammoth. I do not think being a warrior is a path you can choose; I think it is a reality you are simply born into. I admit that this means there are those born to this role who would choose another if they could.

In the BHAGAVAD GITA, the great warrior, Arjuna the son of Indra, the King of the Vedic Gods, finds himself on a battlefield facing friends and teachers. Driving his Chariot is Krsna, who is himself an incarnation of God. Looking at the forces arranged against him, Arjuna doubts, not his ability to fight and win, but whether or not fighting is what he wants to do.

It is Krsna who reminds him that all men die and that those forces standing against him have committed injustices that only violence can resolve. Arjuna still protests that while some Ksatriya[31] must stand and resolve this, he wishes he were not that man. Krsna tells him to man up and do his duty.

If you could choose, that is, if you had to state your preference, would you choose this path?

Musashi and Krsna would tell you that your preferences mean little of anything in light of being who you were born to be. Doubt and the desire to be anything but a warrior only serve to make you a less effective warrior, they do not change what you are. Marcus Aurelius would say, "The lot assigned to every man is suited to him and suits him to itself.[32]"

When we look into the DOKKODO, we see that many of the precepts seem to restate common points or support each other so solidly we wonder why Musashi bothered saying the same things so many ways. In this precept Musashi says to have no preferences at all. In the next, he will say to have no preference in where you live. Everything comes back again and again to "Accept everything just the way it is."

One aspect of this precept that we have to work with is the inherent paradox. To suggest it is best to have no preferences is to prefer that one have no preferences as opposed to having a preference. It is rather like that young Buddhist monk who discards all attachment save his attachment to being unattached.

Another aspect is that attachment to outcome that we discussed in the fifth precept. Musashi is warning us again that to have a preference for a specific

---

[31] The Warrior Caste of Vedic India.
[32] MEDITATIONS III. 4

outcome contaminates the purity of intent that the Way requires. Fight without attachment to the outcome; fight with no preference for life or death, victory or defeat.

When a warrior lifts his spear and engages in battle, it is too late to have a preference. That preference will be a distraction at best. All training and meditation is in the past at that moment and to give thought to past or future in that moment is meaningless.

I think, too, we are again confronted by the Kensei's[33] search for enlightenment and the Do of Walking Alone. This precept is very much in line with Buddhist morals and teachings, more so than anyone who is not a saint or Buddha is likely to readily grasp. Musashi is urging us toward the most arduous path as being the most sincere expression of who we are as warriors because that is what saints and madmen do.

As a zen Buddhist and a swordsman, he was seeking satori, enlightenment, and zanshin, awareness, and mushin, that mystical state of having "no-mind." Operating from those places, pushing conscious thought and decision making aside, allows the swordsman to act more quickly, more decisively and still without error. In the state of mushin, you do not choose to block, you simply block. You do not execute a preference, but simply do what the situation demands you must.

It is not advantageous to prefer life and victory over death and defeat as we have seen. If one can

---

[33] "The Sword-Saint" as Musashi is referred to in Modern Japan.

111

abandon their preference to live in order to simply confront the adversary as the situation demands, one is in harmony with the will of the universe. That is much easier said than done as I think we seek to discard our preference for life and victory only because it stands as a distraction and an obstacle to life and victory.

Musashi has urged us again and again to simply live in accordance with the way things are not wishing they were different, not preferring one situation over another.

As much as I admire Buddhism and Hinduism, I have always been suspicious of any philosophy which suggests I accept the status quo without complaint and simply serve. In India and in the Bible Belt, holy writ is used to remind the poor they should not resent the wealthy but accept what the Gods have wrought. This echoes still in most conservative movements.

This isn't the sort of preference I mean. I think every warrior needs to prefer the Good and want life to be "better" for his family and his tribe and, even, himself. We can argue all day about what "better" means. I would prefer if men taught their sons to be generous and good; if economic injustice were addressed and rectified without resort to theft and violence.

I would prefer it if science eradicated disease and the infirmity that comes with old age. I would prefer it if Mullahs and Imams taught that Allah wants his faithful to live in peace with their neighbors and respect representative democracy as worthy of good men.

But I am not wrapped up in these preferences and very few of them affect my life. I want a cure for my youngest son's diabetes. I want a cure for my sister's cancer[34]. I want my father to be strong and vital for his entire life. But I do not put energy into preferences where my desire means nothing and I accept the heartbreak that comes with living in an imperfect world.

I am not willing to play along with the status quo simply because so many have for so long. Why am I made strong and cunning if not to make the world a better place for my sons and my tribe?

I'd prefer men accepted their nature as warriors and the status quo denounces this loudly and frequently. But my own path is not affected by how my preferences are realized. Many will condemn this small book (or at least give it a bad review on Amazon) and it'll hurt my feelings for a bit, but it won't really impact my own life in any respect.

Again quoting Marcus Aurelius: "Let it make no difference to thee whether thou art cold or warm, if thou art doing thy duty; and whether thou art drowsy or satisfied with sleep; and whether ill spoken of or praised; and whether dying or doing something else."[35]

---

[34] Kathy Louise Hall, ESQ. (17 May 1968 – 6 July 2018) was one of my first training partners as we applied ourselves to the techniques we were exposed to in the KUNG FU TV series and BILLY JACK movies. She fought cancer for 35 years demonstrating daily that one must accept things exactly as they are.

This is part of my Way Alone.

When I saw the classic movie THE LONGEST DAY, I thought of how Musashi might have commented on the decision of the Supreme Allied Command to wait and wait for favorable weather and tides before launching Operation Overlord. They preferred a moonless night with the right tides and an end to the spring rains.

On the one hand, these preferences were essential to the success of the invasion, so maybe it is best to see them as the simple indicators that the time is right. Just as one does not prefer to strike the enemy when he is within range of our weapons, but rather one understands that he cannot strike until that enemy is within range.

We must, however, be cautious that we are not stacking up our preferences and requirements in such a way that we convince ourselves we can never act but only react. Just as we must be willing to act decisively when our intelligence is incomplete, we must be prepared to recognize the time to act is right even when it is not perfect. Our preferences must play no part in our decision to fight.

Musashi is sincere in this urging to accept things as they are without preference, but I think we will see in later precepts he is not confident we can follow the path as he lays it out. Musashi must recognize that we are not saints or Buddhas and we will have preferences. But he wants us to examine our lives and dispense with

---

[35] MEDITATIONS VI. 2

as much extraneous nonsense as we can, hoping, perhaps, we will find ourselves at the point of acceptance of the Mandate of Heaven.

Until then, we can seek ways to limit the need for preference and decision making by simplifying our lives.

One source of stress to modern man is the sheer number of decisions he must make in a day resulting in an inability to choose well quickly, a condition known as "decision fatigue." Modern man is encouraged by his surroundings to have preferences by advertising and the array of options presented by the modern marketplace. For lunch do you want a hamburger or a pizza? McDonalds or Burger King? The Quarter Pounder or the Big Mac? With cheese or without? Advertisers will insist each of these decisions is as vital as any that can be made.

In truth, most of the decisions we have to make are inconsequential and meaningless. In order to keep them from piling up, we can simplify our lives and make those decisions now and never have to confront preferences again. In my wardrobe, I have black shirts and grey shirts, black shorts and white shorts, one pair of shoes, one pair of boots, my tan kilt[36].

The simpler you can make your life, the more inconsequential decisions you can avoid and the closer

---

[36] My mother noticed on the lack of color in my wardrobe and bought me a pair of hot pink shorts for my birthday that I often wear to work out or swim. Sometimes I match them with my Britney Spears t-shirt. Seriously.

you come to the state of having no preferences of that sort.

Perhaps as we travel this way alone, we will come closer and closer to Musashi's teachings. We will have no preference which black t-shirt we wear, then no preference what color shirt we wear, then no preference whether we wear a shirt at all, then we will find ourselves with no preference whether we win or lose but with only the deeds of a man living in accord with his warrior nature without thought.

We will have no preference whether we live or die, win or lose. We will accept things exactly as they are.

Precept Twelve: Be Indifferent To Where You Live

To hear Musashi recommend indifference to where one lives isn't surprising when we remember that he spent his life on the road and died in a cave. Musashi never really had a single residence; he never "lived" anywhere.

Having just advised his pupil to have no preferences in anything at all, why does he now see the need to include this precept?

When I first read this precept, I thought about the holes I lived in during my tours of Iraq and Afghanistan. In Iraq, I had a small corner of a tent, a makeshift desk, a footlocker for a seat[37]. In Afghanistan I had even less. But when I came home, I set up a corner of my apartment very much the same way for the first year or so.

After six years in that apartment, I made a decision to shelve most of my possessions and live under the sky. I, once again, pared my life to the barest necessities of training and fighting. The Musha Shugyo (the Warrior's Pilgrimage) doesn't allow for the accumulation of comforts and niceties and Musashi's entire life was such a journey.

---

[37] During my Afghanistan tour, I had to take a very unpleasant emergency leave. When I returned, I got stuck in Kuwait for a few days. When I finally got back to COP Najil, I lay down and I remember thinking, "I am finally back in my own bed."

While I am on a much longer journey than some, the Roman Stoics advised a certain hardening of the spirit and body through physical discomfort. It was Seneca's advice to "Set aside a certain number of days, during which you shall be content with the scantiest and cheapest fare, with coarse and rough dress..."[38] and Marcus Aurelius added his suggestion of sleeping outdoors or on the floor.

While their intention was the crafting of a body and soul that can easily handle the adversity that results in being without a bed, without a room, without food or clothing, Musashi was living that very life as a ronin. His advice is to adopt a permanent mindset that such things are not to be pursued in the first place.

Musashi was not a Roman Senator conscious of how perilous life is; he was a master less samurai devoted to nothing more than his martial skills and the Way.

I am also reminded of another traveler who wandered his homeland with a group of thugs, teaching virtue and getting into the occasional scrap with the Roman Legions. A man stated his desire to become one of this traveler's followers and was warned: "Foxes have holes and birds have nests, but the Son Of Man has nowhere to lay his head." (Luke 9:58)

Again, Musashi was an extreme individual among extreme individuals. When one studies the arts of war and professes to be a warrior, it doesn't mean he

[38] LETTERS FROM A STOIC by Seneca Letter XVIII, v5,6 (Penguin Classics, 1969)

must then take up the path of the mendicant or the vagabond as well. That Musashi never lived in a house with indoor plumbing and electricity and internet (I have easy access to all three at the moment as I write this) is not an indictment of those luxuries. But it is, I think, vital that we think of them as luxuries and refuse to become dependent on them.

It is crucial that our relationship with any luxury include awareness of that luxury's tendency to weaken us, and we must cultivate an attitude that allows us to forfeit anything that distracts us from our purpose. It is too easy in this modern age to surround ourselves "at home" with impediments to our path[39].

I think, too, that Musashi refers to more than our domicile.

His caution to us to be indifferent to where we live might also include the cities and countries we find ourselves in. I have said before that my own military service was more a devotion to the Way than to my homeland. I now live in the deserts of the American Southwest and I cannot begin to express my love for the land itself. The hot days and the cold nights, the blue sky and the red mountains.

---

[39] This is probably where I should insert Seneca's advice for the third time: "Sleep outside or in the floor, wear thin, rough clothing, eat garbage." It is, I think, the best practical advice there is for a warrior in 21st Century North America where we are surrounded by forces that seek to weaken us and profit by it.

119

But where we live is far less important than how we live. Our lives should be full of gratitude and acceptance for the trials walking the Way alone entails.

It rained for the last two days and I spent much of that time in a tent. When the sun broke through today, I rushed outside and simply laughed with some insane joy that the discomfort was mostly over and a different beauty was claiming my desert again. That joy, the simplicity of my warm tent and the cold winter rain matters to my adherence to the Way. But desert or forest doesn't.

It is difficult, but, as warriors, we must always cultivate a willingness to pick up our weapons and leave all comforts behind to pursue this Way. In the end, we must be indifferent to where we live; indifferent to which rooms, which buildings, which cities, which countries we live in. We must be always ready to move on.

I've discussed elsewhere in this volume my lack of patriotism. As I watch the United States decay into a morass of whining, weak little fucks, I find it difficult to summon up affection for the majority of the people and impossible to summon affection for the state. The noble values of our constitution and the hope it represented are platitudes mouthed by tyrants on one hand and their supplicants on the other.

Its not necessary to list the errors of the past. It isn't necessary to list the glories of the past.

Nothing in this should be taken to imply that I side with those half-educated dimwits (on both sides) who hate the United States and see only her flaws. I am not an expert on political affairs in other countries, but it still seems to me that the US is the most free, "best" country in the world.

I also see that every day the republic slowly turns at the behest of the mob against freedom of conscience and of action. So far as I am a free man and a warrior and one who seeks to serve what is Good, then I cannot consider myself solely a citizen of that state that is turning against me in answer to the whimpers of the weak and frightened children fed on the lies of men who would own us all.

Our passions and our efforts must be guided by reason, not by other passions, and we must accept that our loyalty is to principles and individuals and not the faceless, soulless bureaucracies that govern us.

Being dedicated to ideals and the Good, those warriors who took their oath to defend the constitution seriously, now see it surrounded by enemies in police uniforms and business suits. Any loyalty we feel for those principles leads us now to turn against those systems and bureaucracies created for one purpose, perhaps, but now existing mostly to twist the idea of liberty against itself and foster dependency.

And this is a habit perpetuated equally by the right and the left.

To the extent the warrior is dedicated to the Good, he must recognize that his physical homeland is the ground beneath his feet and nothing more. The accident of our birth does not make us hate or love a state but, rather, reason and our appreciation for the Good. How can any of us look at the current state of affairs in the United States and not realize that soon, she will turn her eyes against us and that every free man will find a place on the gallows while the weak praise the almighty state that it saved them from our dangerous ideas?

We do not hold our country so sacred that when it turns on us we will go meekly. That the men coming for our weapons or for our children are authorized agents of the state means nothing. Just as it meant nothing to those Englishmen turned Americans in April 1775.

As Musashi counsels, we must be indifferent to the fact that our citizenship binds us in any way to those suppress our freedoms at the behest of the mob. That indifference must not be only to the negative things either. Our loyalty and affection must not be a commodity the state can purchase with grants and displays of support. We walk the Way Alone.

Make no mistake; no matter how fiercely you love the republic and its bureaucracies, it does not love you back.

Musonius Rufus, another of those Roman Stoics I won't shut up about, exemplified this precept when he was exiled from Rome despite his position as a Senator. His trial was sprung on him almost unannounced and when he was informed it was underway, he declined to attend because he was on his way to the gym. Then when he was informed he had been found guilty and exiled, he asked if his property had been confiscated. When informed it had not, he shrugged his shoulders and invited his friends to supper at a truck stop along the road to Greece where he lived the rest of his life.[40]

As warriors, as men, as human beings, we will and should cling to our relationships with people even when we cannot cling to the people themselves. We have no caution to be indifferent to our families and our tribes. Carry then, in your breast, the only home and the only homeland you will ever need or serve.

The warrior must constantly be assessing whether his ability to pick up his weapons and move on is hampered by the craving for comforts and attachments to places and things that do not serve him on the Way. Perhaps it is not yet necessary for you to leave behind the place you occupy in this dying empire, but when the time comes, know how well you will be able to do so. Be prepared physically and psychologically.

By its very definition, the Ronin must be a free man and not the servant of the Empire of Nothing or any of its corporate subsidiaries.

---

[40] DISCOURSES I.1.28-30

Precept Thirteen: Do Not Pursue The Taste Of Good Food

The Human Situation has changed a lot in the last 300,000 years and in most ways, it has just gotten easier and easier.

You're still stuck in the body that nature designed for the world as it existed way back then though. That body was designed to be strong and endure hardship, deprivation, injury. Those virtues were essential for everyone in those days when we were far more likely to be hunted by lions than to go on safari and hunt lions from trucks or wolves from helicopters.

The fact that neither of my sons were eaten by bears during their childhood possibly demonstrates this progress was not entirely negative.

The human sense of taste developed as a way to keep our hunter-gatherer ancestors alive. We learned to crave things that were packed in nutrients we needed to function but, most of all, the calories needed to pursue more calories. Calorie dense foods are actually rather rare in nature. Sugar is the most fundamental energy source and we crave it.

Fast forward just over a quarter million years and that instinctive craving for sugar has created an entire industry devoted to supplying us that sugar even though our sedentary lifestyles no longer require it and in quantities our ancestors could never imagine. Another industry arose to tell people how to manage their diets. Millions of dollars pass through the hands of the merchant caste as the mad priests of Madison Avenue exhort the faithful to feed on garbage and then chide them for their obesity and offer to sell them a remedy to that also.

It is commonly said that your body knows what is best for it. That is no longer so when discussing nutrition because the circumstances have changed so much.

Simply feeding your body properly is now an act requiring discipline more than it ever has been. And a full third of Americans are failing with fatal consequences for themselves. The current obesity epidemic is either a symptom of the empire's desire for self extinction or a planned culling of the slave population[41].

The warrior must, in this area of his life, set aside his instincts and study. Or perhaps it would be more accurate to say he must set aside what he has been taught until he knows what his instincts actually cry out for in this regard. The purpose of food is to fuel the body on the warrior's path. Just as we choose our residence and our clothing and our tactics and strategy based on our identity as warriors, so, too, must we study diet and exercise and choose that part of our path based less on what we enjoy and more on what will serve the mission.

---

[41] I'm not really a believer in crazy conspiracy theories but I am a big fan. There are, I think, too many of us. But I think the problem will fix itself in some great event that does not require human participation.

For Musashi, living on the road without an income, the great pleasure of eating was probably found in an adequately full stomach.

Hunger, cold, and sleep deprivation are the tools the US Army's Ranger School uses to exhaust the soldier so that they can train him on an instinctual level. The goal is to exhaust the man and train the beast that emerges. Exhausted, cold, and miserable, the young soldier is then expected to perform on an elite level leading patrols against an OpFor while struggling against his own internal enemies that are urging him to quit, to slow down, to let another bear the burden.

Today, few Americans really understand hunger. Most of us eat two real meals every day and a variety of small, calorie dense snacks. Many eat three meals a day. The weight loss industry suggests you eat five or six times a day and consider it grazing like cattle or some other prey animal.

But there is also a small movement emerging that has discovered the virtues of fasting and intermittent fasting. For the warrior, the value in fasting doesn't lie solely in the physical benefits but also in the psychological benefits. The warrior can accept very little on theory alone, he needs to know that he can function at a very high level even when deprived of sleep or food.

While I refer often to Buddhist teachings when deciphering Musashi's intent, most religious traditions have teachings about fasting. For the warrior, one important bit of advice came from a rabbi who lived in

Roman Occupied Judea 2000 years ago. In the Gospel of Matthew, he is quoted as saying, "When you fast, do not look somber…but when you fast, put oil on your head and wash your face so it will not be obvious to others that you are fasting…" (Matthew 6:16-18 edited)

The significance of this teaching isn't just for the purposes of holiness, but also a reminder that, as Sun Tzu taught, when we are weak we must appear strong. We must never let our team, our family, or our adversary suspect we are not at our most dangerous. We must not only be strong when hungry, but we must appear strong. This is another benefit of intermittent fasting and any fasting program: we learn to be proficient and appear proficient even when deprived of sleep and food.

Having said all of that, I again think it necessary to talk about what Musashi didn't say; he didn't say "Scorn the taste of good food."

For the warrior, food is about nutrition. Taste is a secondary consideration at most. I'm not one of those fanatics who lives off of rice and chicken and water. I've mentioned in other essays that my sons and I find ourselves at Chuck E Cheese from time to time.

Just as the DOKKODO is about the ronin's relationship to life, each precept can be examined as a comment on a relationship with some aspect of life. For the fat merchant pursuing the goals of fat merchants[42], the taste of food is one of the rewards his life choices delivers. That is his relationship with food.

---

[42] I have no idea what those goals really are.

The warrior's relationship with food, as put forward by Musashi in this precept, is concerned with fueling his training and struggle. As long as that is the crux of your relationship with food, the crux of your relationship with the world, you are following the Way.

Read about nutrition and study your own habits and set aside what doesn't make you stronger. I recommend Arthur De Vany's THE NEW EVOLUTION DIET, Loren Cordain's THE PALEO DIET, Mark Sisson's THE NEW PRIMAL BLUEPRINT, and Ori Hofmekler's THE WARRIOR DIET and THE ANTI-ESTROGENIC DIET. Then do what you think is best.

Precept Fourteen: Do Not Hold Onto Possessions You No Longer Need

Again, Musashi isn't writing for a 21st Century Suburban beneficiary of the merchant caste; he is writing as a man who lived his life on the road to another man who will probably live his life on the road. Musashi lived the majority of his life with his weapons, the clothes on his back and a few things in his bedroll. He carried his life on his back and in his scabbard.

This probably made divesting himself of the possessions he did not need much easier than it is for you and me.

You and I have greatly different ideas what it is to "need" something than Musashi did. And we aren't wrong, the world has changed and much of the simplicity of Musashi's life won't be available again until after the Empire dies. He lived in a cave. If you resolved to live in a cave, the state would hunt you down for vagrancy or not filing your property taxes.

Even so, modern man has exaggerated his sense of what he needs. I need my truck. It is my shelter, my storage, my way to work. It is 17 years old. Many would suggest I need a new truck. I do need new engine mounts and a new exhaust system. I wonder if I need an older truck so I can do more of the work on it myself. And yet, there are thousands of homeless veterans who prove daily that I do not actually NEED my truck for survival.

Only you can determine what you actually need. Does it follow you must throw away the rest?

Musashi doesn't say to give away those possessions you no longer need. He says to "not hold onto possessions you no longer need." It may seem like there is no difference, but in the world we live in, there must be. We surround ourselves with things we do not need. We must learn not to be attached to them, not to hold onto them, so that when we must part with them, we can do so quickly and easily.

It is very much in line with suggestions that we seek out discomfort so we can be satisfied that we are capable of functioning if such discomfort is forced on us by circumstance. We must learn how to function without our possessions just in case we are one day stripped of them.

This precept is also, perhaps, a call to live as simply as one can. Avoid attachment to unnecessary possessions so that you are not affected by their loss. The warrior cannot be willing to give attention and care to anything that distracts him from the Way. The warrior must take care that he does not allow his possessions to possess him instead.

I think that such attachment to things is artificial for the human animal in the first place. Perhaps this opinion can be condemned as a naïve view of humanity, but I think generosity and non-attachment are the native state of mankind and that greed and covetousness are artificial constructs. There is very little evidence of social engineering designed to help people live with less and a great deal of effort expended to encourage people to want more and then to supply those wants.

At the same time, the warrior must be a man who cares for his few possessions with skill and diligence. I am not attached to my truck any more than I must be. I seek not to be possessed by it. That does not mean my oldest son and I do not spend hours changing the water pump. We clean and maintain our weapons slavishly almost, making the activity a bonding experience. Perhaps every possession we claim MUST possess us to an extent and that is why we must be so very careful what possessions we commit to.

My favorite example of people being tied too tightly to the material circumstances of their lives is seen in how so many people purchase weapons. Every time I go into a gun store, I see some aspirant warrior handling the latest M4-AR15 clone while a salesman explains to him the benefits of the barrel and the frame and the optics and so on.

At that customer's level of proficiency, none of those extra expenses will contribute anything to his accuracy. He simply isn't so skilled that an extra gimmick on his rifle will bring him a single MOA's worth of accuracy. He doesn't need a $1600 AR, he needs a $400 AR and $1000 worth of training courses.

But training is difficult and you first have to admit you have a gap in your skillset and that can be so difficult for men. He doesn't want to have to learn and practice, he wants to possess the ability to reach out with his weapon and he thinks that can be purchased and held in his hands.

He doesn't need the fancy scope, the tightly twisted barrel, the fancy gear. But he becomes attached to them even before their purchase and that attachment becomes an obstacle to his progress as a shooter.

If he could let go of or avoid that attachment to those possessions, his path would become easier and more sincere.

All people desire comfort and to have "enough" that they can set aside worry over food and security. But the desire for enough becomes corrupted when merchants teach the sheep that there is never enough and that comfort is not luxury and that there is always more to want, more to need.

If a poor warrior approaches the state and asks for help living simply, he'll draw blank stares. If he asks for more money to live a more material life, he'll be handed forms and put in line.

This isn't a new state of affairs. The classics of Japanese literature and the Romans, too, are full of financial advice for the soldier and citizen not to over spend and not to become a slave to fashion and commerce.

In the warrior's quest to live an authentic life in accordance with "the way things really are", he must examine his own life and his own psyche. Enlightenment might be nothing more than stripping away the mask overlaid on a man's true self until that self is again what lives and expresses itself without being filtered by the artificial layers of materialist culture and fear.

Many of those layers are tied more tightly to us through our possessions.

Musashi did not seek out the fanciest katana made by the latest, greatest sword smith. The most skilled samurai to ever lift a weapon fought many of his duels with a wooden sword and often carved that sword on the field immediately prior to his duel. He was known to say that a wooden sword was invincible[43].

A wooden sword and a $400 AR15 become invincible, perhaps, when the warrior lifting them understands that what he is; his skill and his mindset, far outweighs the quality of the tool in importance.

Our young marksman with his $1600 rifle will lack this understanding and his performance will suffer when deprived of his toys and gimmicks, even when those toys did not offer any real benefit in his hands.

Cody Lundin has demonstrated that even a soldier's boots can be viewed with an eye toward such "need." In one episode of his survival TV show[44] he went about barefoot in sub freezing temperatures. He remarked then that being barefoot was an essential part of his own training, observing that in many cases, a

---

[43] I can't find a source for this and I've been saying it for years. That search continues. At any rate, we know he fought several of his duels with a wooden sword and did so to test and demonstrate his spirit as well as his skill.

[44] It was on DUAL SURVIVAL and I can't find the episode. The footnotes for this chapter suck.

warrior might have millions of dollars worth of training but be worthless when deprived of his hundred dollar boots.

We hold on to what we need. We let go of what we do not.

More than most, we know the difference.

For many, attachment to one's possessions is an attribute of ego. Some men derive a sense of identity from the car they drive, the neighborhood they live in, the name on their suits or shoes[45].

The warrior derives his identity from his purpose, the cause he fights for, his training, his role as defender. Even the skill set he possesses becomes a tool for serving his cause and not his identity. This is all part of this attribute of letting go of what is not needed.

While this may not be inherent in Musashi's precept, there is also the almost obvious idea of generosity. Generosity is one of the cornerstones of my own Code. Only a coward clings to the wealth he accumulates. A warrior understands that his strengths can fill his coffers again and again. This confidence is the root of all generosity.

Not clinging to what I do not need, I am free to give gifts to those who do still need such things. This

---

[45] Whether it is the insistence that one only wears the most expensive Salvatore Ferragamo Oxfords or the refusal to wear Nikes because they picked the wrong guy to sponsor. The purpose of shoes is to protect your feet (and make yourself appear civilized when in court) and if you are asking them to do more than that, you are probably wrapped too tight for the way of the ronin.

generosity is impossible without acknowledging this precept.

The warrior must constantly analyze which material attachments are rooted in need and which are rooted in mere sentiment. While I do not advocate divesting yourself of sentimental belongings, start to set them aside in your heart so that your clinging does not give them power over you. Carefully consider the place new acquisitions have in your adherence to the Way.

Precept Fifteen: Do Not Act Following Customary Beliefs

While we see Musashi's way of life as extreme, it was not unknown in medieval Japan. It was common enough to have a name: Musha Shugyo, the Warrior's Pilgrimage. His society had room for that warrior who spent his life wandering the land, challenging other warriors, seeking to perfect his skill and risking his life to do so.

While it might not have been the most common path that a samurai spent his life on, it was not a rejection of his society's customary beliefs like it would be for us today. The fact that you know Musashi's name and are reading this book indicates you have already put aside many of the Empire's customary beliefs.

This precept was one of the lessons Musashi learned while on that pilgrimage. Musashi must have seen the failure of those relying on custom and the successes of those acting outside of customary belief. One belief he rejected on this pilgrimage was that the katana was most properly used in two hands. He developed instead a style of fighting with his long sword in one hand and his smaller sword in the other.

It's hard for those of us in the modern west to understand the significance of this rejection of style. It's the same sort of revolution that occurred when men began holding pistols with both hands.

He developed this two sword style. He named it. He wrote a book about it. He taught it to students.

There is no evidence he ever used it in a duel. Every story we have about his duels has him wielding one sword (sometimes a wooden sword) with two hands.

Perhaps the lesson here is the key to understanding this precept. A certain degree of unpredictability is of great use to the warrior, especially the ronin fighting alone. By demonstrating that he had developed this new revolutionary style, but still adhering to the old style, Musashi created this uncertainty in his opponent. He is capable of acting according to customary beliefs, and he is capable of acting without consideration of those beliefs.

This precept isn't designed to create mindless adolescent rebels who reject customary beliefs with no intent beyond that rejection. To reject a belief rooted in the experience of warriors who came before you is no easy thing. Much of what we learn from our teachers and our society is perfectly accurate, it can be the foundation around which the rest of the Way is constructed.

That seems especially difficult to grasp fully in these days of rampant commercialism and materialism. Our society has no room for the warrior walking alone. In the midst of a generation condemning the generations that came before it, proposing that an ancient generation may have known truths we have forgotten is itself the rejection of a customary belief.

The mere fact that we recognize ourselves as warriors and devote ourselves to this path that does not pursue monetary wealth, physical comfort and moral numbness makes us out to be extremists. Many of us reject the teachings of the dying empire, its meaningless churches and its hollow institutions that serve no purpose beyond the empire and the accumulation of power for its masters.

Rejecting churches that serve the empire instead of the gods, and universities that serve any doctrine other than truth and wisdom requires you to reject the beliefs customary in this age in favor of the higher purposes such institutions were created to fulfill.

We then seek these older paths, traditional martial arts, a morality more in tune with the ancient world than the modern, and skills that haven't been practical since the Wild West was tamed. But even then, we cannot accept at face value the beliefs held by Ueshiba, Kano, Fairbain, or even Musashi. We must question and explore everything. We may not ever base our actions on the customary beliefs or traditional teachings of our forbears.

My first exposure to jujitsu was Inazo Nitobe's book BUSHIDO: THE SOUL OF JAPAN[46]. It was 1983 and the ninja craze was just beginning to catch traction. I was an 18 year old college freshman and desperate to study an authentic martial art. I was fortunate enough to find a jujitsu program at a nearby community center and studied there for two years before enlisting.

---

[46] BUSHIDO, THE SAMURAI CODE OF JAPAN by Nitobe, Inazo (tr Alexander Bennett) Tuttle Publishing 2019 is the version I have read most recently.

The jujitsu we studied was, according to our instructor, a Japanese martial art. We learned the basics of unarmed fighting; the same punching and kicking and blocking that form the core of most martial arts. Then we learned a few self-defense tricks; escapes from grabs and rough situations. These tricks always involved taking control of the attacker in some way. When pushed, we'd pull. When pulled, we'd push.

We also learned to throw a standing opponent to the ground once we'd established that control over him. This was the crux of jujitsu as I knew it.

I go into this detail because there is no doubt that this training was authentic. But fifty years before I studied this Japanese martial art in Dallas, Texas, a Brazilian man had begun his studies in jujitsu and his family would take these teachings in a direction that most Japanese had not anticipated; focusing on sudden take-downs instead of throws and manipulations of joints and limbs once on the ground.

Today, there are many who do not even know that jujitsu is a Japanese art, and we have all studied the techniques and strategies of that Brazilian family. They have proven the efficacy of their art so thoroughly that there are many schools of "Brazilian Jujitsu" that do not even carry the Gracie name. For the sport-fighter, and arguably for every sincere student of war, it is essential to have at least a passing familiarity with the ground fighting developed in Brazil as an offshoot to the Japanese Martial Arts.

We do not act based solely on customary beliefs.

Just as Musashi's two sword style was a dramatic departure from traditional kenjitsu ryu, so Gracie jujitsu is a dramatic departure from traditional jujitsu ryu. We embrace these differences because experience and observation prove they are effective and prowess is more precious than tradition.

The warrior does not reject customary belief just for the sake of juvenile rebellion. But he also does not cling to it for the sake of tradition and habit. The need for this principle in our martial studies may seem obvious. But the warrior applies this precept to his entire life, his society, and every mode of thought.

Seeing the emptiness in our modern society, we keep what we find useful. We reject the rest. Studying history and philosophy, we keep what is useful. We reject the rest. Never do we rest and allow habit to take root or any beliefs left unexamined to become the basis for our actions.

This must also include our own beliefs.

We must not allow our beliefs to become so unquestioned that we find ourselves acting based on nothing more significant than "this is what has worked for me in the past." We must be constantly training, studying, learning, growing so that new understandings come to replace old beliefs. And each new understanding must be accepted as vulnerable to even newer understandings.

Perhaps we could say that we do not act following customary beliefs because we do not hold any customary beliefs. Nowhere does our mind rest on an idea but moves constantly instead, deeper and deeper so that every action is based on an understanding more refined than yesterday's mere belief.

It will sometimes happen that after research and deliberation and experimentation we discover that a customary belief is true exactly as we were taught it. But that it is customary and "what we were taught" will never be the reason we hold that belief.

Of course, we analyze our beliefs and our societies but we must always push further. We will often read something we know we disagree with and seek out a single new truth. We must honestly examine our actions and our habits and determine where we do, in fact, act without thought based on nothing more than customary belief.

Most importantly, the ronin must be responsible for his own beliefs. His code might be rooted in the teachings of long dead rabbis, ronin samurai, Athenian philosophers. But it is his alone.

The fact that we study Musashi does not mean we commit to his ideas before we make those ideas our own. We take them in, digest them, update them to apply to a world of firearms and night vision.

We take in the creeds of our various armed forces even though we no longer answer to them. We create our code and are, therefore, even more responsible for our adherence to it. Our Way does not permit another man (or an Empire) to force his ethics and his customs on us.

This Way of Walking Alone is, in the end, our own Way, given birth and voice by the individual warrior following even when it has roots in antiquity.

This point will be especially important when we come to the last of Musashi's precepts.

Precept Sixteen: Do Not Collect Weapons Or Train With Weapons Beyond What Is Useful

Given Musashi's previous admonition about property and attachment, the first part of this precept seems straightforward. If you're walking the way alone, owning more weapons than you can access easily is overkill, it weakens you. Anything that weakens you must be set aside. It's that easy.

It's almost foolish to tell the modern day warrior (no irony intended, I include myself and my sons in this indictment) not to collect weapons. Especially when we add in that "beyond what is useful" clause. My son's Mauser will probably never see actual battle again, but he continues investing money in it building a sweet, sweet sniper rifle. But is it useful?

Every warrior I know is a romantic. This rifle my son builds was carried by a loyal subject of the Kaiser in 1914, probably again by a soldier fighting in the Wehrmacht (carried on the Western Front against my son's Great Grandfather and his brothers who landed on 8 June with the Second Infantry) then by a young man who carved his name in the stock during the wars against communism which followed. Simply holding this rifle puts my son in touch with the warrior spirit.

It is that spirit that makes a man a warrior, not his weapons. Those weapons, as the saying goes, are only tools. It is the individual with a well trained hand and a disciplined mind who is the weapon. When we begin asking ourselves what is useful, we must address that. What possession and what level of training contribute to the mind and body of the weapon himself?

With this in mind, any training that enhances our effectiveness in battle is useful and nothing is more vital than to train the mind and the spirit. The training I do with sword and shield is intended as training for body and spirit. It is, in many respects, the same childish play I have always engaged in, pretending to be a knight or legionnaire or gladiator or viking or samurai, and not the serious training I do on the dojo mat or the range or the gym, because I have few illusions I will ever rely on the sword for my life.

It is still useful, perhaps even vital, because it touches something inside me and draws me closer to the Way. No amount of skill or fitness can compensate for a simple willingness to fight. The spirit must be trained first. Then the mind. Then the body. Then the skill set[47].

If the spirit to follow the way is absent, it will be impossible to properly discipline the mind. If the mind is not resolute, no plan to train the body for war will be

---

[47] While I am absolutely convinced of this order of development, there is nothing more pathetic than that fat kid who insists he has trained a warrior's spirit (and possibly even mind) but isn't fit enough to pass the physical exam to enlist. Worse still is that kid who boasts of his prowess and his warrior nature but declines to enlist because "there is no honor in modern war." There are lots of good reasons not to enlist. That you're too good for it isn't one of them.

pursued diligently enough to matter. If the body is not capable, skills will remain elusive.

Just as one has to consider carefully and allocate their limited time to training in those disciplines that most prepare the warrior for the fight, it is also necessary to consider how much time can be applied to training. There is a point at which training becomes over training and the warrior begins undoing the benefits gained. This can be very difficult for the novice who is eager, even anxious, to learn everything NOW.

It's important from time to time to train when physically exhausted so the experience isn't completely alien. This is one of the premises behind the US Army's Ranger School. Ranger students are kept underfed and sleep deprived in order to teach them to operate under these conditions. Exhaust the man; train the beast that emerges.

But exhaustion leads to mistakes and practicing mistakes can undo the forms and lessons learned. It is vital to find the point at which training becomes overtraining and approach it cautiously.

When I was first exposed to the DOKKODO many years ago, this precept was worded or translated as "Do not make a cult of your weaponry" and I am going to address that idea, which is somewhat different from "Do not overtrain" and "Do not collect weapons."

In the GO RIN NO SHO, Musashi counseled us to train with and become familiar with all weapons. It is prudent to understand the tools your adversary uses and how they are employed in order to counter and defeat them. Once familiar with weapons, it is necessary for the warrior to choose which tools best serve his purpose and begin to pursue excellence within a smaller selection.

Even then, he must never idolize his tools to the point where brand names become incantations. A sword is very much a sword, a spear is very much a spear. A handgun...a rifle...every tool is what it is and no more[48]. It is, again, the warrior's spirit and mind that make them weapons.

As we do not collect weapons, we will probably find we possess and practice with a few select pieces. In my career in law enforcement and the military, I have carried a variety of handguns, both revolvers and automatics. I can argue the pros and cons of the Beretta M9 and the Sig Sauer P229 gleefully. Put either in my hand and I will use it as the tool it was designed to be. I carry a Beretta 96A1. It's no better or worse than any other gun. It's just different. It is not sacred. But it is mine. In my hand, this weapon is more dangerous to the adversary than another because I am so familiar with it.

Another might carry a Glock[49] or a Taurus or any other weapon. It is the warrior who makes the difference. While some weapons might be better made than others, more accurized, better sighted, it is, in the

---

[48] Unless you shoot a Glock. It seems Glock shooters are trained that the first part of clearing a malfunction is to say, "That's never happened before." (I'm just kidding...for the most part.)
[49] See footnote 2.

end, the hand holding it that makes it a weapon. It is always the contest of spirits that decides victory.

I recommend, as did Musashi, that we become familiar with as many weapons as possible and become familiar with those principles that allow us to handle one handgun or rifle as we would any other. It is necessary to become familiar with different weapons so we know that an AK fires from the open bolt and an AR fires from the closed bolt. But both require the same aim and trigger squeeze.

Then we must train diligently with the weapons we carry so that their handling becomes second nature.

Again keeping in mind that over training results in making mistakes second nature.

The warrior must know why he owns the weapons at his disposal. Whether it is for the practicality of carrying concealed or the comfort of a shotgun for home defense or simply holding an old Mauser to feel some of what the men who carried it before him felt, he understands why that weapon has a place in his arsenal. Any tool that does not positively make the warrior a stronger weapon, is set aside.

Precept Seventeen: Do Not Fear Death

Again and again we have said that the warrior does nothing that does not make him stronger, more efficient. Fearing death or fearing anything for that matter is not likely to make us better warriors.

But we have so little control over our fears. It's easy to say we do not fear death because we all imagine death to be very far off. But if you have a fear of spiders or the letter "K", you can see how impossible it is to simply decide not to fear anything.

My youngest son was afraid to jump in the pool for the longest time. He couldn't swim very well. The pool is so big and he was so small. He was, of course, afraid of dying.

It was impossible to convince him without experience that he would be okay.

Aristotle taught that one learns to be brave by doing things that require courage[50]. He was firmly convinced the virtues could be taught and that courage was no exception. I am not sure what we should call that iota of courage required to push us into that confrontation where we can practice this virtue.

My son and I developed a short litany. I would ask him, "What do we do when we can't be brave?" And he would answer, "Pretend to be brave." Embracing the philosophy of "Fake It Until You Make It" he slowly

---

[50] NICOMACHEAN ETHICS Book II. Paragraph 1

conquered that fear only by experiencing that jumping into the pool did not lead to extinction.

In doing so, I am not certain he actually impacted his natural fear of death at all.

We overcome our fear of death not by denying it but by accepting it and it is impossible to experience death and, upon our miraculous return, have lost our fear of it. More, as my son learned that jumping into the pool didn't mean extinction, we must be prepared for the possibility that complete extinction is exactly what death is. We can fear the unknown; we cannot deny our fear until we have accepted it and comes to terms with it.

In the TV series SPARTACUS, the gladiator trainer we will later learn is Onomaeus gives some new recruits their initial instruction on what it means to be a warrior and their new relationship with death. He says, "A gladiator does not fear death. He embraces it, caresses it, fucks it. Each time he enters the arena, he slips his cock into the mouth of the beast and prays to thrust home before the jaws snap shut."[51]

A little graphic, but perhaps demonstrates one way a warrior might confront the inevitability of his death in such a way as to chase away fear.

Bruce Lee agreed. In a line he improvised for the TV series LONGSTREET, in which he played the hero's martial arts instructor, he said, "Like everyone else, you want to learn the way to win but never to accept the

---

[51] https://youtu.be/FYRdgKLqK4M SPARTACUS Season One Episode Two

way to lose. To accept defeat, to learn to die is to be liberated from it. So when tomorrow comes, you must free your ambitious mind and learn the art of dying."[52]

In the end, though, a fear of death will not serve a warrior and so death must be accepted. This idea has been taught again and again. The pop culture literati from Paulo Coelho and M Scott Peck have written of death as that constant companion that advises us and gives life meaning. The HAGAKURE had stated this much more completely as an admonition about a samurai's virtue by "setting one's heart right every morning and evening, one is able to live as though his body were already dead. His whole life will be without blame."

Death is inevitable we are reminded again and again. Keeping in mind day and night that the memory of our deeds and characters will outlast us, we can begin to live with the idea of being prepared to die and to kill others. This lesson is part of the dharma taught to Arjuna by Krsna in the BHAGAVAD GITA. The impermanence of your life should free the warrior from any fear save the fear of dishonor and the fear of being unrighteous.

This is much easier said than done, however.

Marcus Aurelius, with whom I have been spending far too much time lately, gave us this advice: "It is a vulgar but still a useful help towards contempt of death, to pass in review those who have tenaciously stuck to life.[53]" Working in a VA hospital, I had this point

---

[52] https://youtu.be/fWanEKlbfJk

driven home on more than a few occasions, seeing those men, once strong and cunning, reduced to feeble shadows. It is not polite to suggest that one would rather die than live as so many of the elderly do.

In the ILIAD, the old man Nestor chides the Acheans for their unwillingness to charge forth and fight Hector. He says he would do so were it not for his advanced age and claims that, in his day, men were braver and better than the younger generation he now counsels. It all sounds so familiar when I speak to those young men today who have no feeling for the sword. But when he finishes his address, Agamemnon asks Nestor how, if he was so brave, he got to be so old.

And that is one indictment that stays with me. I know my limits, but even now, after half a century, I seek the courage and activity that my own death will not come from natural causes (save being shot by a jealous husband MIGHT be considered "natural causes" for a cavalryman) but that instead my death will be evidence that I never gave up living my life in favor of having it slip away slowly.

My fear of death is curbed by having seen in explicit detail what life becomes if one refuses to let it go.

A man's life is a story. It has a beginning, a middle and an end. Just like a Hollywood script, it's probable that the story of a man's life will make sense; the middle flows from the beginning and the end could only come from a few different directions.

---

[53] MEDITATIONS IV. 50

If you spend your life behind a bottle and watching the game every Sunday, your end will probably not be a beautiful one. The sedentary man gives little or no thought to his death, being bored already with his wasted life. When death comes, it crawls in quietly, slowly, the pills and medical visits seeming a mere nuisance at first then culminating with a breathing corpse in an antiseptic hospital room.

In the United States today, the idea of a beautiful death is alien to most people. If life can be beautiful and should be beautiful, then why should a good fitting death not be desired also? What cowardice drives that man who seeks extreme measures hoping to stave off the inevitable day? Why is the modern man so willing, even eager, to outlive his body and even his mind?

Seeking to accept that death comes for us all and that the fear of death gives us nothing of value, it becomes possible to consider that a good death at the right time is a thing to be desired. The Norse thought that the only path to Valhalla was a death in battle. The worst fate that could befall a man was to die in his bed. In this day, that man dies in a hospital bed surrounded by relatives who just want it over with.

To again quote a Stoic, it was Marcus Aurelius who pointed out to us that we should not fear death because it is inevitable, and, more, we should consider what it means that Death is the will of the Universe for all things. How then can it be bad?[54]

---

[54] MEDITATIONS IV.3

When I was a freshman in college, Dr Michael Platt asked our literature class three questions and whether he intended it or not, 35 years later, those three questions still haunt me. The first of them (or was it the last?) was "How do you want to die?"

Which of us, reading Stephen Pressfield's GATES OF FIRE, doesn't wish he had such a fate awaiting him? Which of us, when signing the papers of our enlistment, didn't secretly write the citation on his posthumous Medal of Honor as well?

I don't recall meeting anyone who actually wanted to die in any given day's fighting, but we all expected such a death at some point. We couldn't imagine any other. If you hold to your courage and refuse to stop fighting, you will eventually lose. If you risk anything, and a warrior must risk everything, you will eventually lose everything.

If you are a warrior, you should expect your death to flow seamlessly from your life.

Is there anyone anywhere who actively hopes to avoid Death until he is old and infirm, drooling, senile? Is there anywhere a man who wants to die in a hospital and not outdoors in the fields where he spent his life or at his desk writing, reading, making war on Ignorance and defending the Good or behind his podium passing on the lessons his battles have taught him?

That man who struggles and fights and seeks adventure as a student of the Way taunts death, perhaps, and death always responds.

Let us then treat this precept as we treated others. Whether we fear death or not, let us resolve that such fear will not make our decisions. We will set our minds right every morning and every evening and we will train and study and behave as though we understood that we are mortal.

We will let death counsel us, but only counsel us to advance and build; never to shrink back in hopes of immortality. We will act as though we are brave even we cannot be.

Precept Eighteen: Do Not Seek To Possess Either Goods Or Fiefs For Your Old Age

Again it is Musashi's advice that we not become attached to the world and that we seek nothing but the Way itself. Even if we incur the obligations of wives and children, our duty to them must be encompassed within the Way or it becomes a pulling away from our place as warriors as described in a previous precept.

I found it interesting that this precept comes directly after an admonition not to fear death. If we have been successful at putting aside our fear of death and we have lived lives of adventure, never backing down when the Good is challenged, then we probably won't live to that point where we cannot provide for ourselves and must instead rely on "goods and fiefs" that we came to possess when younger men.

When we think of death, we think of the pain of passing from injury or illness, we think of losing our loved ones, we think of leaving forever the only world we know. These are the fears the ronin must set aside. Setting aside the fear of death, we live more interesting lives, more complete and more full.

If a man has instead spent his life in pursuit of goods and position, then his fear of death will probably be heightened by the certainty of losing those things. The merchant covets and collects and then becomes possessed by his possessions, his fear of bankruptcy pushing him even as his greed pulls him into a way of life that is seldom heroic. To his "natural" fear of death is added the weight of knowing none of treasures will accompany him into the grave. His death and the bankruptcy that comes with the grave are certain and a heavier weight, perhaps, than that burden the ronin carries for the Death that acts as an advisor and not a tormentor.

Still, a man might find himself in possession of fiefs and goods as a result of pursuing the Way. Just as the warrior is passionate but not guided by passion, so might the ronin eschew greed and without stepping from the Way find himself in possession of fortunes and fiefs[55]. But true to his nature as a warrior, he will still remain unattached to these goods and fiefs that he accepted but did not seek or lust after. Remaining unattached to his possessions, his fear of death will be held in virtue of having "nothing to lose."

There is nothing wrong with wanting to leave fortunes behind for our children (and our retainers and students) when Death finds us. But the Way prompts us instead to live in consideration of the stories and name we will leave behind. The Banker leaves his sons a monetary fortune. The warrior leaves behind his tools and the stories of his deeds for his children[56].

---

[55] COMBAT FINANCE by Neddenriep, Kurt. Wiley Publishing, 2014. LTC Neddenriep was the SCO of the 1/221st CAV, NVNG, while also a Senior Vice President of a major investment firm. He's a great example of how a warrior can follow the Way and become financially successful also.

[56] I inherited nothing financially upon my Grandfather's death. But much of what you read in this commentary is only made possible by the example he set as a working man, as a husband and father,

Like so many other precepts, we can see that this one speaks of intention more than anything else. The desire for political power and wealth is incompatible with the Way. That doesn't mean that one on the Way won't find himself wealthy and in a position of influence. But that energy a man puts into his pursuit of such things is time away from the Way and could make it impossible to progress.

It seems natural, perhaps, for a warrior to want to progress in rank. When I was a soldier, the army had policies designed to force soldiers to seek promotion or be put out. It was inconceivable that one might wish to stay a private or a skilled corporal. As a result, soldiers were pushed not to their highest level of competence, but their lowest level of incompetence.

A young soldier who knew nothing was expected to chase rank and position rather than prowess. The ronin is spared this burden.

This doesn't excuse an experienced soldier from accepting the role of trainer and mentor when called upon. But even then, this duty should not be taken in expectation of reward. Rank should carry no privileges but only responsibility and burden.

The obligation a warrior owes his superiors and his juniors and the army itself when he is enlisted could

---

as a hunter and fisherman, as a builder. The last moments my Grandfather spent at home were spent walking around the house making a list of projects he had to finish when he left the hospital. The last words I ever said to him were, "I'll be back" and his last words to me were, "I'll be here." I would not trade that for silver.

all serve to pull him into politics and away from the Way. This is another reason why a man like Musashi would walk alone. I think the experiences of serving in an army contributed to my pursuit of the Way but was only a diversion from the Way of Walking Alone.

The goal of an army is very seldom to promote the Way among the warriors serving in its ranks. In many cases, I think adherence to the Way would run counter to the goals of an army and the state that army serves. The empire needs us to each be committed to its values of commerce and material excess. The empire needs you to be dedicated to property and fiefs in your old age and in your youth.

Those who benefit from your pursuit of possessions and status, those who convince you during million dollar Super Bowl commercials that THEY are the suppliers of the good life want you to commit to a life of comfort and ease. They whisper incessantly that possessions and fiefs are yours for the taking if you'll just submit to them and pass your days struggling for currency and paying your taxes.

There is little time for the pursuit of prowess and honor when you have to be at work on Monday in order to buy a new car and the right beer and pay the rent by the 3rd of the month. The merchants will seek to convince you that the right beer and the right car are the proper path to honor and sex and love.

In this sense, it seems that the warrior must choose between the Way and a fief even without Musashi's advice.

One notable exception was my experience with the Nevada National Guard. The officers and senior enlisted men there were not dependent on the state for their livelihood. They considered the military a calling, a duty, but not a profession. That is: they sought to attain the pinnacles of glory and prowess but did not owe their daily bread to the empire.

Many of them grew wealthy from their own pursuits, but none were required to subvert their own natures and their own progress on the Way to the demands of their military service.

Several months ago, I was listening to a local talk radio host during an interview with one of the city's wealthiest men. This man was controversial at the time because he had made a statement about having "enough." He had recently been outed as an anonymous philanthropist. (I myself had been benefitted from this anonymous largesse in the form of a gift card worth $500 given to many members of the Nevada National Guard at Christmas.)

During this interview, he explained again what he had said and what he meant. He had billions and had decided years ago that he had more wealth than he could spend in a lifetime and that his wealth continued to increase and so he was determined to give much of it away. He was also calling on other wealthy men to consider doing the same.

Now, he wasn't advocating that the state be involved at all; not interested in any socialist forced re-distribution of wealth. And he wasn't advocating that anyone retire to a monastery and give up the good life his wealth provided him. But he felt he could give away fortunes and improve the life of his community without harming himself.

Again and again he said "I have enough; we have enough."

Finally, a caller incensed at the idea that anyone might have enough, accused him of being a communist or a hippie and demanded to know who had the right to determine how much is "enough".

The question could only be asked by a slave, a serf of the Empire of Nothing. Was it not apparent that the man had decided for himself how much was enough? Wasn't he suggesting that other men ask themselves freely to consider how much was enough without advocating that any of them sell their cars or favorite horse? But the Empire rebels against the idea that any man might decide that he wanted to make the lives of others better when he could continue to amass a meaningless fortune.

I would think any warrior grasps the idea that glory is better than comfort and being a "despiser of gold", as the Norse Sagas name a generous man, would be preferable to whatever emotional state leads one to amass fortunes that cannot be spent and cannot be held on to after death.

One idea popular in some financial circles is that one should plan their retirement in such a way as to "die broke[57]." While the experts speak of annuities and

---

[57] DIE BROKE: A RADICAL FOUR PART FINANCIAL PLAN by Pollan,

401K, I remember reading that someone planning to die broke should consider giving away as gifts those things that might have been left to a loved one in a will.

Musashi had no real family. The student he wrote the DOKKODO for was his only heir and I'm not certain he left him anything but his teachings and his name[58]. That same situation might very well be the case for many of us. But many of us, too, will find ourselves concerned with what we leave materially for our families when we pass. This concern existed in Musashi's time also even though it wasn't a personal concern for him.

Retirement for the samurai usually took the form of a full withdrawal from the affairs of civic and family life and taking the robes and vows of a monk, as we saw with Yamamoto "Jocho" Tsunetomo, the author of HAGAKURE, which was composed during that retirement to a monastery. Having a fief and lands and the obligations of a daimyo would have meant very little when it was time to shave one's head and begin preparing for the next life.

It is necessary, perhaps, in this age to plan for one's retirement and, while I personally can think of no retirement better than a hermit's cottage at a monastery, such planning often requires consideration of those financially dependent on us.

But even so, we take nothing with us when we die and the legacy we leave is not enhanced by the

Stephen and Mark Levine. Harper Business. 1998.
[58] Don't you wish we knew where his swords went when he died?

zeros in our bank account. Whatever wealth we gather while alive should be discarded and given back to our family and our tribe before our death.

Instead of fiefs and castles, we could leave behind parks and schools, hospitals and scholarships. I think the warrior should do these things in his own name, and the names of those he would honor before he dies instead of leaving such things to attorneys and clerks who squabble after estates. Dying broke is the best service we can grant our communities and our heirs.

I think that as we train our sons to follow the Way as we have, it would do a disservice and, perhaps, appear insincere to gather wealth and leave that to them on our passing. They, too, must be prepared to make their own way from day to day. Instead of hearing your will read and learning they are now the possessors of your fortune, you should give those gifts from your own hand while still alive.

The treasures we leave behind should be memory and a few emotional tokens given during life. Time spent together is the best purchase a warrior can make for his children's inheritance and it is not cheap. You will not need a fief in your old age.

Resolved to follow the Way, especially the Way of Walking Alone, the warrior should expect to make his own way from day to day and receive neither recognition in the form of position and possessions nor to see old age. Attachment to either will inevitably pull the warrior away from the Way.

Precept Nineteen: Respect Buddha And The Gods Without Counting On Their Help

That one should respect the Gods (and the saints and the Buddhas) is a given in the same way that one should respect their parents. I'm not willing at this point to get into any discussion about parental neglect or the individual circumstances where one might have legitimate reason to hold their own parents in contempt. We are all flawed and that includes our parents. Regardless of those flaws, in all but the worst of circumstances, we owe our very lives to adults who came before us and called us their child.

Nor am I interested in any discussion about whether there is a God. Insert your beliefs here. If when I say "the Gods" you think I am describing the impersonal functions of an impersonal universe, that's okay. I do not have a dog in that fight.

The Gods (or the "One True God", or "nature", if you must) occupy for the world the same position that parents do for the individual: creators and caretakers, divine parents, patrons of heroes. The respect due the Gods should seem obvious. The saints and the Buddhas occupy much the same place, being men who sought the divine and attained some favor.

Musashi, being Buddhist, recognizes that he and his students owe respect to the Divine, but then insists we not count on the Divine for aid.

Despite the stories that dominate western religious literature, warriors have long known that reliance upon the Divine was never enough to attain victory. While we know Napoleon never said, "God is on the side with the biggest battalions" we also know that Voltaire did once say, "God is not on the side of the big battalions but on the side of those who shoot best." (Napoleon may have replied "God is on the side with the best artillery.")

The lesson here is that the Gods do as they will and seek their own ends and purposes. A man can do nothing but train and prepare. But history indicates that being well trained, well equipped and well prepared secures victory more than any faithful reliance on the divine.

More, it is the nature of warriors to rely on their own strengths and prowess rather than any other's anyway. David might praise his God for teaching his hands to make war, but he carried a sword and shield as well. Regardless of the odds, a warrior expects to die on his feet fighting and not kneeling in front of an altar begging for his life.

As Marcus Aurelius advised, "In truth, we ought not pray at all."[59]

Among the Norse, there were two concepts related to the idea of Destiny: Wyrd and Orlog. Wyrd is the great big fabric of the world's fate. Orlog is that part of the fabric that concerns the individual and, while changing Wyrd would require the cooperation of entire populations, Orlog can be affected by the actions and intentions of the individual. Wyrd might demand that

---

[59] MEDITATIONS V. 7

nations go to war. Whether the individual goes and whether he prevails is determined by his Orlog and that is determined by how he has trained and dedicated himself to prowess.

Respect the divine. Seek virtue and justice. But instead of being one of those who depends on the divine for his support, the warrior seeks to be the Hand of Heaven and the Fist of God.

I once heard a story about reliance on the divine that speaks to the soul of a warrior walking the Way Alone.

A man raised among the faithful saw the suffering and terror in their world and waited patiently for his God to intervene. A lifetime passed and the man lost his faith, taking the injustice and suffering present in the world as evidence that there was no God.

Upon his death, he found himself before the Holy One and was understandably shocked. He immediately exploded at the almighty.

"How dare you stand in judgement? You who abandoned us to the adversary! There was hunger and violence and sorrow and hurt and you abandoned us! You did nothing!"

His God was stunned as so few would had ever dared to speak to him so. But that stunned silence was quickly replaced by righteous anger. "I did nothing?" demanded the almighty. "I did nothing? I saw famine and I saw violence and I saw suffering and I saw a lonely world in need of justice and mercy..."

"AND SO I SENT YOU!"

The warrior does not seek to be the recipient of aid, but to be the personification of that aid. A child in some third world shithole prays to her God that He will rescue her father from a tyrant's death squad and an SF ODA[60] slips across a border in the night to answer that prayer.

The warrior does not seek to benefit from another's generosity but to be the source of comfort and largesse to those he defends.

This is especially so in early Buddhism and Zen Buddhism. In these sects, there was less homage paid to the Buddha as a divine figure who might grant aid. The emphasize was on recognizing that the practitioner himself is a Buddha and need only follow the Buddha's teachings and example in order to realize this and "manifest" it his own life.

In Buddhist thought, it is impossible to rely on the Buddhas without relying on yourself. You have an obligation to discover your true nature and that true nature is the divine and your own Buddha nature. Zen is not a study of the divine as something "out there" but, as taught by the Zen Master Dogen, "To study the Dharma is to study the self.[61]"

---

[60] Special Forces Operational Detachment Alpha-an "A-team" for those of you who didn't know. They're kinda like Navy SEALS but talk a lot less shit.

[61] THE ESSENTIAL DOGEN: WRITINGS OF THE GREAT ZEN MASTER by Eihei Dogen (edited by Tanahashi, Kazuaki and Levitt, Peter), SHAMBALA, 2013

It is out of that respect for the divine that we, as warriors, act on the behalf of the divine as we understand it best.

We might beseech the Gods for wisdom, but we will read and study. We might beg the Gods for strength, but we do so at the gym and in the training hall. We might pray for help, but we will make ourselves ready to act as though no such help were coming.

We respect the Buddhas and the Gods. Or perhaps we honor our place in an impersonal universe. But we recognize that what we become and what becomes of us is a result of our choices and our own will.

Precept Twenty: You May Abandon Your Own Body, But You Must Preserve Your Honor

It's common to hear people lament (or boast) that honor has no place in the modern age. I hear it from warrior-wannabes who excuse their cowardice with the complaint that they are concerned with honor but somehow that honor is missing now from the world and the military and modern wars and so they will not serve. I hear it from merchants who boast that their greed is the only virtue and that the proof is found in the poverty of "honorable" men that they have manipulated. I hear it from warriors who stare stunned at both of these positions.

Whenever this discussion about Honor comes up, I soon confront the difficult task of defining Honor. I find every definition scribbled in dictionaries to be unsatisfying. "Honor is keeping your word." "No, that's honesty." "Honor is being reliable." "No, that's integrity." " Honor is doing the right thing." "No, that's justice."

All of these concepts have an impact on honor, but honor is itself a "something else." Honor is the foundation of virtue, the sincerity that lies under every virtuous deed.

Honor is the commitment that some principles are so important to the warrior, that he would accept extinction sooner than he would violate those principles.

The details of one's personal code of conduct, the arguable points of right and wrong, are almost immaterial.

A common example (at least in sophomore philosophy classes) used to show how grey morality can be revolves around an act of theft. We all know theft is wrong. However, every thief rationalizes the deed as an act that he was somehow entitled to commit. It is always somehow the victim's fault or the wrong is simply negated by circumstance.

If a child is starving, is it morally wrong to steal a loaf of bread to feed that child? Now...let me assert again...our discussion is not about which side of this debate an honorable warrior might take, only that we find in his dedication to that stance his honor. Honor is, again, the idea that we would choose extinction before we would choose to abandon our code.

For that warrior who holds property rights to be the most sacred thing, honor demands he refrain from theft and undergo the pain of watching a child starve. For that warrior who values life, honor demands he steal. Either of these warriors must be willing to lose their life as a result of their actions rather than see their principles violated.

A man need not consider his deeds to be flawless, morally unquestionable, or legal to see that they are the demands of honor. The world is imperfect and there are many times the choices we are presented with do not permit an untainted deed.

The true nightmare occurs when one is committed to a code that holds monstrous misunderstandings of the Good. There are cultures that hold a woman's chastity to be more valuable than her life. A rape victim might be murdered by her father or brothers because the loss of her virginity is a stain on the family honor. The media has come to call these "Honor Killings."

I think its fucking insane.

While so many then use this example to discredit notions of Honor, I see it as a corruption of Honor rooted in the corruption of the moral code being adhered to.

"Honor Killings" and the Code of Silence observed by mafioso and street gangs[62] imply an "Honor Group", an intimate group of near equals with a common code and loyalty to each other. Every veteran knew a soldier who wasn't a bad guy, maybe, but he just wasn't a good soldier. That soldier was seen as less-honorable than others because he had accepted an obligation to the group (his unit, the army) that he wasn't living up to.

As a ronin, Musashi wasn't a member of such an honor group, unless we count that entire culture of

---

[62] This Code of Silence is an indictment of that sort of Honor only found in groups. Anyone can see where remaining silent when questioned by an enemy to protect your brothers is a virtue. But among criminals, this code is observed mostly in its violation. Thugs almost always snitch. But pushing this code that will not be observed, leaders of criminal organizations are only attempting to control those under them.

Samurai. Other Samurai, those dedicated to a Daimyo and a Clan, would absolutely have seen Musashi as being less honorable because of his masterless status.

For a man to be honorable, his code must be more important than his life. This is the meaning behind this assertion. If your path, if your way, your Way, is not worth your life, then it is not the right Way.

You will die. Your body will be abandoned. You cannot preserve it.

But you can preserve your honor and, therefore, you must.

This leads us to the last of Musashi's 21 precepts:

Precept Twenty-One: Never Stray From The Way

There is, perhaps, much in these precepts that can be debated and argued against.

There is, certainly, much in my commentary on these precepts that can be debated and argued against.

Only you know what set you on this path and what precepts, what commandments, what laws, what principles guide you.

Take what you will, discard what does not serve you on the Way.

But never stray from the Way.

AFTERWORD

But then again...

On at least three separate occasions, the greatest Ronin to ever live, Miyamoto Musashi, approached a lord and applied to enter his service. At least one of those lords declined his application because his other samurai did not think they could live in peace with a man of Musashi's reputation.

In his essay "Belonging Is Becoming", found in BECOMING THE BARBARIAN, Jack Donovan puts forth a convincing argument that the "rugged individualist" is a man of no consequence whose antics and programs neither serve nor disturb the Empire. He argues that only in small groups, tribal groups, can the individual have any meaning. In his pursuit of personal freedom, the ronin accepts "statistical irrelevance."

I think he's right.

I also think we have to be okay with this.

Several times in this commentary I mentioned family and tribe. And it must be kept in mind that Musashi is writing a letter to his student. A man with students and adopted sons is not exactly alone. It is not hypocrisy; the core of pursuing one's own identity is found along two paths: the Way Alone and that way of serving one's tribe and the Good.

In Musashi's admonition to have no preference to where one lives, we encounter the idea that, perhaps, we are not condemned to be formed by our society but that we might instead meet men who become brothers and form tribes based on who we are rather than being created by social pressures. The moral relativist argues that one sees the Good only through the lens of his society. Perhaps now we can turn that upside down and create new tribes at the fringes of the empire dedicated to radical new visions of the Good and virtue.

In medieval Japan, most ronin were seeking new lords to serve. Some, failing at this, became bandits and joined gangs. Very few took to the Musha Shugyo and lived as Musashi did. I do not think the end of my journey will find me again wielding a spear or a black rifle for a lord.

But I hope it finds me firmly ensconced with family and tribe, my children and their children on the edge of the empire's remnants.

That young knight headed to Camelot so he can serve the Good and only the Good might have many interesting adventures, but he only accomplishes something meaningful and lasting when he is bonded to his fellow knights around Arthur's Round Table.

But in this empire, it isn't easy to find tribes. The men in my own community who feel as I do must be numerous (Man is bred for war, remember?) but they are apparently so beaten and so consumed by the identity forced on them by the empire that I do not see them often.

There are dozens of books and an entire marketing scheme built around the idea of men needing tribes and being "bros." Joining these tribes and uniting with these men in search of prosperity and belonging is no more difficult than paying your few thousand dollars and attending their next "warrior seminar."

Real tribes and real relationships built around a warrior ethos are a little more difficult.

And that is part of why I wrote this.

Between now and the time you are initiated into a tribe, or a gang of bandits, or take refuge in a monastery, or are appointed into a Daimyo's service, you are alone. It is okay to be alone like the Preacher in Clint Eastwood's PALE RIDER: drift in, commit to a community, do some good, confront and destroy an oppressive evil, wander off.

But it is better, I think, to wander in, commit to a tribe, do some good, confront and destroy an oppressive evil, form relationships, raise children, leave a legacy. Be one of the ancestors worshipped and remembered in the shadows of a distant future.

Accept things exactly as they are.

I welcome your comments, questions, complaints, even insults and accusations.

I can most easily be reached at:

AmericanRonin.TheWayAlone@gmail.com

I can also be followed on twitter:

@stormcrow762

Made in the USA
Monee, IL
26 February 2021

61423556R00098